Bright Gems for His Crown

*Ninety-three Daily Devotionals to Help Build
Qualities of Character in Children*

BRIGHT GEMS FOR HIS CROWN

Ninety-three Daily Devotionals
to Help Build Qualities of Character in Children

MAXINE RANDALL

Belleville, Ontario, Canada

Bright Gems for His Crown

Copyright © 2003, Maxine Randall

All Scripture quotations, unless otherwise specified, are taken from the *New King James Version*. Copyright © 1979, 1980, 1982. Thomas Nelson Inc., Publishers.

"Count Your Blessings" hymn by Johnson Oatman (1856-1922).

Permission to use "Two and One" and "The Golden Rule" poems granted by A Beka Book, Pensacola Christian College.

National Library of Canada Cataloguing in Publication

Randall, Maxine, 1941-
    Bright gems for His crown / Maxine Randall.

ISBN 1-55306-507-7.—ISBN 1-55306-509-3 (LSI ed.)

    1. Christian children—Prayer-books and devotions—English.
I. Title.

BV4870.R35 2003   242'.62   C2003-900126-1

**For more information or
to order additional copies, please contact:**

Maxine Randall
17 Elridge Lane
Willingboro, NJ 08046 USA

Guardian Books is an imprint of *Essence Publishing*.
For more information, contact:
20 Hanna Court, Belleville, Ontario, Canada K8P 5J2.
Phone: 1-800-238-6376. Fax: (613) 962-3055.
E-mail: publishing@essencegroup.com
Internet: www.essencegroup.com

Special thanks to the following children:

*Our daughter, Neesie Randall (age 8),
who, while working through the devotionals, offered
suggestions and insights and even caught some mistakes.
May we see fruit in her life.*

*Our good friend, Daniel Noor (age 7), who was a very
willing tester of a sample of the devotionals. We appreciate
the comments from him and his family.*

*Two other friends, Trisha DeGroot (age 10)
and Jessica Bier (age 10), who also tested samples
and gave perspectives from an older point of view.*

*Also special thanks to our friend, Nadia Noor,
and our daughter, Beverly Randall, for their very capable
help in proofreading the manuscript.*

*Thanks also to my friend, Mrs. Jean Minck, for reading
through and making corrections to the final manuscript. Her
time and help has been much appreciated.*

Important Words to Parents

This book was originally written as a publication to be offered to customers of our small family home business called *Speakable Gifts*. The Lord has now laid it on our hearts to try to put it into the hands of as many children as we can. So we have had it published, and we present it to you and your child(ren) with much love. Our purpose for providing these devotionals is twofold: First, we are trying to provide a helpful start for many children of what we hope will be a life-long practice of personal daily devotions. Second, we are hopeful that we will be providing a forum for discussion between parents and their children regarding Biblical issues and practical character development. We do not consider this book to be an exhaustive doctrinal study for children. However, there is some doctrine sprinkled throughout, and we have tried to cover, in some way, all of the Ten Commandments. Please keep in mind that our primary purpose is to encourage the development of character qualities. We are trying to speak to the heart of your child, so we would also ask that you forgive us if on a few occasions we are not strict about grammar rules.

We are making some assumptions. We are assuming that, for the most part, children using these devotionals are in homes in which they are already learning spiritual truths and that they are involved in churches and Sunday schools that support these teachings. Another thing we would like to mention is that, for the sake of convenience, most of our references to the home have to do with situations where there are two parents living in the household. While we sincerely believe this to be God's design for the family, be assured that we recognize that there are many other types of situations, such as single parent families and some instances where a child or children are being brought up by godly grandparents or other relatives. Please remember that we are also speaking to all of you who are in these situations when we use the term "parents."

How to Use this Book

This book has been structured in such a way so that your child can do the devotionals on his or her own. However, we want to stress the importance of parental oversight. Please read the devotionals before your child does, so that you can see what he or she will be doing. You might want to do this on a weekly basis. Or, if you prefer, you could do the devotionals together, especially if the child is younger. Each day, have your child read the introductory thoughts and the prayer for that date, and then do the devotional for that month. Take note that the introductory thoughts and the prayer are read every month on that particular date, so that each of them is read three times while using this book. Then, for the month's devotional, the Scripture passage is read, the discussion of the topic (Part A) is read, and then the quick response question is answered. Part B is an activity that should be done later in the day. These activities are, of course, optional, but they do help make the point of the day's devotional more clear to your youngster. We ask that you please determine whether or not you need to supervise these activities (see "Note to Parents" on the section entitled "About the Activities").

There are three months of devotionals. Month 1 is the month in which you start. If, for example, you begin in April, your child would start on the first of April and do the devotionals for Month 1. Then, in May, he will read the devotionals for Month 2 and so on. Thirty-one days have been allowed for in each month. For months with thirty days or less, or any other days that your child may miss, you might decide to have them completed later. Some families may want to cover extra devotionals in family worship.

Use these devotionals in a way that works best for you and your child, and we are quite sure that our God will bless all of the efforts that go into it—yours and ours. We pray that *He* will receive all of the glory in your child's life. It is our prayer that this child of yours will indeed be a bright gem for His crown—beginning now!

~Maxine Randall

Dear Children,

Did you know that Jesus is coming again and will gather His jewels for His kingdom? Did you know that these jewels are those whom He loves and who belong to Him? Are *you* one of His jewels whom He will gather when He comes? If you are, then that would mean that you love the Lord Jesus. Those who love their Redeemer are special treasures to Him and must shine brightly for Him. That means that they must live for Him, and be the kind of person *He* wants them to be. As young as you may be, you can ask God to help you love Him and shine for Him. You can ask Him to help you to know what it means to be a precious jewel for His crown. I hope the devotionals in this book will help you learn how to be a shining light in this world. Maybe you will be one of the pure jewels He will someday gather when He comes. You can start right now being a bright gem for the Savior. You can do these devotionals by yourself, but you will need to talk about many of the things with your parents. You should do one devotional each day and you should read the thoughts and prayer for that day of the month. Your mom or dad will help you get started. The devotionals will last for three months. I hope that they will help you to begin to be the bright gem we just talked about. I hope that each day, while you read the verses, answer the questions, and do the various activities, you will be learning that you can be a bright gem for Jesus by...

1. Knowing God
2. Confessing Sin
3. Loving Jesus
4. Learning God's Word
5. Praying
6. Loving Others
7. Having Self-Control
8. Obeying Your Parents
9. Being Kind
10. Watching Your Tongue
11. Being a Helper
12. Working Hard
13. Trusting God
14. Telling the Truth
15. Being Responsible
16. Having Courage
17. Caring
18. Giving Cheerfully
19. Doing Your Best
20. Being Humble
21. Keeping from Evil
22. Being Loyal
23. Being Thankful
24. Being Unselfish
25. Not Being Envious
26. Forgiving Others
27. Not Complaining
28. Being Content
29. Having Good Manners
30. Being a Witness
31. Following the Shepherd

One more thing: Don't forget to pray! Each month, remember to look at the prayer suggested for that day and let it be *your* prayer. After all, how can you live for Jesus without His help? And may He bless you richly, now and always.

In Christian Love,
"Aunt" Maxine

About the Activities

The following items will be helpful to have for the activities. You may have most of them in your home already:

Pencils and pens
Crayons, colored pencils, markers
Playdough—homemade or purchased
Medium-sized chalkboard or dry-erase board
Colored chalk or dry erase markers
Scissors, glue, stickers
Construction paper
Plain index cards, 4 x 6 size
Dolls, stuffed animals or beanies
A few books of Aesop's Fables*
A good hymnal

* You can usually find plenty of copies of these fables at the library. You will find that there are a variety of interpretations of the different fables, depending upon the publication.

This means you may have to adapt some of them a little to the subject at hand. If you want to make sure that you have copies of the particular fables we refer to in this book, they are listed here for your information:

The Tortoise and the Eagle
The Ant and the Grasshopper
The Boy Who Cried Wolf
The Wolf and the Crane
The Dog in the Manger
The Raven and the Swan
The Dog and the Shadow (The Dog Carrying Meat)

Note to Parents: We have tried to include activities that have little or no potential for injury or damage, but as you know, when children are involved, we should never take that completely for granted. That is why it is so important that all of the activities be reviewed by parents ahead of time. In many cases, the activity should be supervised by a responsible adult. Parents need to make that determination. If there is any activity which parents feel is inappropriate or unsuitable for their child, they should by all means skip it. The publisher and the author accept no responsibility for any injury or damage caused by the child's participation in any of these activities.

When He Cometh

When He cometh, when He cometh
    To make up His jewels
All His jewels, precious jewels
    His loved and His own.

He will gather, He will gather
    The gems for His kingdom,
All the pure ones, all the bright ones,
    His loved and His own.

Little children, little children
    Who love their Redeemer
Are the jewels, precious jewels,
    His loved and His own.

Like the stars of the morning,
His bright crown adorning,
They shall shine in their beauty,
Bright gems for His crown.

~ William O. Cushing

The LORD their God will save
them in that day,
As the flock of His people.
For they shall be like the
Jewels of a crown.

Zechariah 9:16

15

Knowing God

In the very beginning of the Bible (Genesis 1), we learn that Almighty God is the Creator of all things. Everything in the world belongs to Him. You belong to Him. We all belong to Him. Everything and everyone are under His control and rule. He is the One whom we should want to please and obey. We cannot live for God our Creator unless we know who He is and what He wants us to do. He wants each and every one of us to seek Him (try to find Him) as hard as we can. On the first day of each month, we will learn some important things about our great God.

When You Pray

After each month's devotional for the first day of the month, ask that our great God will help you to know Him better.

Devotionals for Each Month

1. God is Holy
2. God is Spirit
3. God Knows All Things

MONTH 1

God is Holy

Exodus 3:1–6

A. The first thing we need to remember is that God is very **holy**. This means that He is pure and is all goodness. He never sins—He always does what is right. In your Bible reading, Moses saw a bush that was burning. Moses went to look at the bush because, even though it was on fire, it did not burn up. When he went to look at the bush, a voice spoke to him. It was the voice of God. Moses was told to take off his sandals because he was standing on holy ground. Moses was afraid to look at God, so he hid his face. That is because God is so great, so glorious and so very holy. This is the first of many devotionals that we will do together. We think that this is a good place to start, don't you agree? Moses knew that God was holy. We want to make sure that you know it, too.

Write True or False:

The ground where Moses was standing was holy because the holy God was there. _____

B. Ask your family to sing the hymn "Holy, Holy, Holy" tonight before you go to bed. Ask your parents to explain what some of the words mean. When you get in bed, pray that God will help you to understand how we sinners can come into the presence of such a holy God. We will talk more about that tomorrow and the next day.

MONTH 2

God is Spirit

John 4:24; Exodus 33:20

A. As we think about what God is like, we need to know that God is spirit and He does not have a body like we do. We cannot see a spirit, so we cannot see God. Even though we cannot see Him, God is very, very real. He sees *us* at all times and He takes care of us. We may not be able to know what He *looks* like, but we know that He is great and powerful. We can see all that He has made and learn about Him and, even better, we can read the Bible and learn about Him. And best of all, He sent His Son to show us what He is like.

Circle the right answer:
I can draw a picture of God. (Yes / No)

B. Later today, play "Hide and Seek" with someone who is good at hiding. You be the seeker (make sure the other person hides in places that are okay with your dad or mom). Think about this after you find the person who was hiding: Did you need to see that other person to find him or her? Do you need to see God to find Him? Did He see you when you were seeking? Did He see the person who was hiding? Does He see you all the time?

MONTH 3

God Knows All Things

Genesis 4:8–11; Proverbs 15:3

A. Cain did a very evil thing when he killed his brother. Do you think maybe he thought no one saw him? Well, God knew exactly what he had done. That is because God sees and knows all things. He knows everything there is to know about each and every one of us. He knows when we do what is right and when we do what is wrong. So, of course, when Cain did that wicked deed, God knew it. Because God knows everything, He hears what we say and even knows what we think about. How does that make you feel? We hope that Jesus is always pleased with all the things He knows about you.

Circle the sentence that is true:

(a) Sometimes we can hide things from God.

(b) Nothing can be hidden from God.

B. During your playtime today, pretend that you are a school teacher. You can teach some other children or you can teach some dolls or stuffed animals. Teach some of the things you have been learning in your schoolwork. You

23

might even want to make charts or flashcards and use a chalkboard. While you are teaching, think about why God never has to go to school. Again, what does God know about *you*?

Confessing Sin

I t is a very sad thing that our hearts are so sinful. It is very sad that sin is so strong in us that we find it very hard to obey God. When we disobey God's laws or rules in any way, that is **sin**. We know that we *should* obey Him—He is the One who made us and takes care of us. We also know that we cannot glorify Him unless we love Him and do what He commands. But the sad thing is that we are **sinners**. It all started with Adam and Eve, the first people that God made. Adam and Eve sinned when they disobeyed God and ate the fruit that He told them *not* to eat. Then, because of this, they became sinners and sin spoiled the world God had made. After that, they could not obey as they should and the same was true of all their children. Now, all babies are born with sin in their hearts. All children who want to be gathered when Jesus comes must understand what it means to confess their sins.

When You Pray

Pray to God each and every day: "Lord, I know that I need your forgiveness daily. Teach me to confess my sin. Whenever I am tempted, please help me to seek your help. Help me to love You and obey You. Amen."

Devotionals for Each Month

1. The Unsaved Must Confess Sin
2. The Saved Must Confess Sin
3. Confess to God and to Others

MONTH 1

The Unsaved Must Confess Sin

Luke 18:9–14

A. Jesus told this story to teach something. Jesus wanted the people He was talking to, to know that everyone is a sinner. The problem is that some people do not think about how sinful they are—they are too proud. The Pharisee in this story was like that. He was bragging about himself when he prayed. The other man, the tax collector (the publican), *did* think about how sinful he was. He cried out to God for mercy. He **confessed** to God that he was a sinner. That means that he admitted it to God. Now, which man was forgiven? You are right, it was the one who confessed his sins. People who want to be saved must confess their sins to God. They must **repent**, or turn away from their sins. That means they should ask God to forgive them of their sins and when He does, they should try to live for Jesus from then on. You, too, must repent of your sins and come to Jesus if you want to be saved. It is the same for everyone.

Circle the right answer:

God forgave (the Pharisee / the tax collector).

27

B. When your parents have time later on today, act out the story for them. Show them first how the Pharisee acted. Say some of the things he said when he prayed. Next, show how the tax collector acted. Say what he said. Tell your parents which man was forgiven and why. Ask them to explain to you better why sinners must confess their sin. Ask them to explain to you what it means to repent.

MONTH 2

The Saved Must Confess Sin

Psalm 51:1–4; 10

A. This is part of a prayer of David, King of Israel. Why was he praying this way? It is because he had sinned a great sin. He had taken another man's wife and he had arranged it so that the other man was killed in a battle. King David was a child of God. How could he do such a thing? It is because even God's children still have sin remaining in their hearts. Sometimes they still want to please themselves rather than God. Whenever a child of God sins, God knows it. We cannot hide our sins from God. God did not like what David did and sent a prophet to him. The prophet told David that God was going to punish him. David felt very sorry for what he had done and asked God to forgive him. Even though God did punish David, He forgave him and David did not stop being His child. When someone truly loves Jesus, that person will be sorry for his sins. He will confess them to God, and God will forgive him.

Write true or false:

God's children are perfect and do not sin. _____

B. Do you wash your hands when you get them dirty or before you eat? When you wash your hands today, think about how you can get a clean heart after you sin. Remember, if you belong to Jesus, God forgives you when you confess your sins to Him, even though you may still have to be disciplined. Also remember this: wash your hands with soap and water to get them clean; wash your hair with shampoo to keep it clean; bathe your body to keep your skin clean; brush your teeth with toothpaste to help them stay nice and clean and free from germs; but Jesus is the only One who can make your heart clean. You must belong to Him, trust Him, and love Him. Talk more to your parents about it. Ask them to also explain why you might sometimes have to be disciplined even after confessing your sin and being forgiven for it.

MONTH 3

Confess to God
and to Others

Luke 15:11–19

A. In today's Bible reading, you read one of the stories that Jesus told. This was one of His parables. Like all of His parables, Jesus was using a story to teach the people something about God. This story was about a young man who went away from home. He had little concern for his father and even though he had a good home, he did not want to be there. He was supposed to get some money someday, but he did not want to wait for it. So he begged his father to give him the money early, and when he got it, he left home. He left his family and went on his own so that he could do just what he wanted to do. But after he left, hard times came. He wasted away his money and, after a lot of trouble, he began to feel bad about what he had done. He knew he had sinned. So then, he did the right thing: he went back to his father and confessed his sin. We hope that you will do the same thing. Not only had he sinned against God, but he had sinned against his father also. If you sin, confess it to God and also confess to those you sin against. Always try to obey your parents, but if you ever do disobey, remember to confess your sin to them as well as to God.

31

Circle the right answer:

**The young man did right when he (left home /
confessed).**

B. If you have time today, write a story about a child
who disobeys his parents. Make it a pretend story that
you make up yourself. In your story, after you tell about what
the child does wrong, tell what you think should happen after
that. Tell what you think the child should say to his parents.
Show your story to your mom or dad. Ask them if they think
the child in your story did the right thing in the end.

Loving Jesus

We have thought about our great God and we have thought about our sinful hearts. We have thought about our need to confess our sins. Today we need to think about Jesus. As we think about Jesus, you need to know that God in His greatness and goodness *must* punish sin. This is what is just and right. When your parents punish you when you are not obedient, they are doing what is right. And God is doing right when He punishes sinners. Now, you need to understand that Jesus has something to do with that. It is the third day of the month. Is it cold winter? Is it hot summer? Maybe it is a lovely fall or spring day. Maybe it is raining. Whatever the weather is like, today we think about something very, very important—we think about the love of God in His Son, the Lord Jesus. As you do all of the pages in this book and learn all of the ways you can be a bright gem, none of these things will really mean anything if you do not love Jesus.

When You Pray

Pray that these devotionals will help God to show you your sin and His love in the Lord Jesus.

Devotionals for Each Month

1. Jesus is the Way to God
2. We Must be Born Again
3. Jesus Saves All Kinds of People

MONTH 1

Jesus is the Way to God

Matthew 1:18–25

A. When we think about how holy God is and how we are sinners, we do not feel that we can come near to God. But Jesus is God's Son. He is also holy because He, too, is God. God sent the Lord Jesus to earth to be our Savior. Jesus died on the cross to save sinners. Even though He had no sin Himself, He took the punishment that sinners deserved. He took the punishment in their place. He did this for all those who would trust in Him and believe in Him and what He has done for them on the cross. For those who do believe and trust the Lord Jesus as their Savior, God will forgive their sins and save them for Jesus' sake. Then, and only then, will they be able to go to God and someday have a home in Heaven. We hope and pray that Jesus is your Savior. If He is not, we hope that He soon will be.

Write true or false:

We cannot go to Heaven without loving Jesus.

_____

B. Read the words to the hymn "Thou Dost Reign on High" (sometimes it is called "Thou Didst Leave Thy Throne"). It is a Christmas song. Maybe your family could sing it together even if it is summer. Talk with your family about why Jesus was born and what He did with His life. What was the main reason that He came? What does the hymn say about your heart? Is this true?

MONTH 2

We Must Be Born Again

John 3:1–8

A. Because God is so very, very great, there are so many things we can learn about Him. We can study and study and study about Him all our lives and there will always be more things we can learn. In fact, we will never be able to understand everything about Him. One thing that will be hard for us to understand is the fact that even though there is only one God, He is three Persons. He is God the Father, who is in Heaven, God the Son, who came to earth to save us, and God the Holy Spirit, who works in our hearts.

We have already talked several times about our sinful hearts. How can we go to Heaven with our sinful hearts? We have talked about confessing sin and last month we talked about Jesus as the only way to God. But it is very important we understand that we need new hearts if we are to go to Heaven. We need new hearts if we are to be able to love Jesus. God the Holy Spirit must do this. He can give us hearts that hate our sins, love Jesus and want to please God. When the Holy Spirit does this, we are **born again**. That is what Jesus was telling Nicodemus in your Bible reading.

Write the answer:

Who alone can change your heart? _____

B. Look at a photo of a newborn baby, if you happen to have any around your house. It could be a photo of a brother or sister or someone else. Maybe the photo could be of you when you were first born. What do newborn babies look like? Ask a parent to explain to you what people look like when they are born again.

MONTH 3

Jesus Saves All Kinds of People

Matthew 19:13–15; Acts 10:34–35

A. When the Lord Jesus came to earth, He came to live a sinless life, and then to give His life for sinful people. He gave His life by dying on the cross. But just as God had planned, Jesus did not stay dead. He rose from the dead and He is still alive, and will always be alive, to save those who will come to Him. He is ready and willing to save sinful people of all ages, all colors, and from all countries. Some people care too much about how old people are or what they look like. Jesus is not like that. You can come to Him if you are young or old, rich or poor, or of any color or nation.

Circle the right answer:

Does all this mean that children can come to Jesus?
(Yes / No)

B. With your colored pencils and construction paper, draw a picture of a lot of children. Make their faces many different colors. Do not make them blue or green or

39

purple or other silly colors, but colors like the ones people really are. Now, mark a big "X" on any of these children who *cannot* come to Jesus. What color are you? Can *you* come to Jesus?

Learning God's Word

The best way we can learn about God and His Son Jesus is by reading the Bible. Learning God's Word is the only way to know just what He wants us to do and just how He wants us to live. We need to love the Bible, read it every day and be thankful for it. We need to ask God the Holy Spirit to help us to understand it when we read it and memorize it. The Bible is the very best book in the whole world. If you want to shine brightly for Jesus, then you must learn the Bible.

When You Pray

Here is a prayer for these devotionals: "Almighty God, help me to listen to your Word and to obey it. Help me to understand it so that I may do what pleases You. In Jesus Name, Amen."

Devotionals for Each Month

1. God is the Author of the Bible
2. God Speaks to Us in His Word
3. Love God's Word

MONTH 1

God is the Author of the Bible

2 Timothy 3:16–17

A. Because the words of the Bible are God's Words, we can say that God is the **Author** of the Bible. An **author** is someone who writes something or creates something. Since God is the Author of the Bible, He is also the One who can help us to understand it. We need to pray to Him for His help when we read it. We call the Bible the "Holy Bible" because God is Holy. The Bible is a wonderful book. God wrote it for our good. In it, we learn about God, His ways and His works. In it, we learn about His Son. And in it, we learn about ourselves. It is only in the Bible that we learn what God requires of us as human beings.

Do you like to read? Do you have a favorite author whose books you like a lot? It is very good to read. We can learn many things. It is good if you *enjoy* reading. No matter how many books you read in a day, please be sure that each day you read the Book written by God, the Author who cares more about you than anyone else.

43

Circle the best answer:

Because the words of the Bible are God's words, all of the words are (happy / true).

B. During playtime or crafttime, get a piece of colored paper. It's a rectangle, isn't it? From one of the shorter sides, cut a strip about two inches wide. Then cut another strip the same size. Out of one of the strips, make a bookmark for one of your reading books. Write down the name of the author and the name of the book. Draw pictures on the bookmark or draw a border with your colored pencils, crayons, or markers. Then, with the other strip, make a bookmark for your Bible. Don't forget to write down the name of the Author!

MONTH 2

God Speaks to Us in His Word

1 Samuel 3:1–10; 2 Peter 1:21

A. There were times when God talked to people by actually speaking to them. He also sent prophets to His people to tell them things He wanted them to know. God spoke to a young boy named Samuel one night. You just read about that. God spoke to Samuel and told him things. After that, God sent Samuel as a prophet to tell His people things He wanted them to know and to do. God talked to others from time to time, like Abraham and Moses. God also sent many others who were prophets to talk to the people. Now we have His Word, the Bible. God chose men to write down His words. These words are the words of the Bible. Like we said last month, the Bible tells us about God and His Son and about our sin. It tells us how we are to live for God. Whenever you read the Bible, God is speaking to you. Be sure to listen carefully. You listen to the Bible when you pay attention to what it says, and try your best to *do* what it says.

Write down the name of the book in which God speaks to people: _____

45

B. Ask a parent or an older brother or sister to help you make a recording. Ask if you may have a cassette tape with nothing on it. Have them set up a tape recorder for you to record with. For your recording, read something from the Bible that you like a lot. Maybe you could start reading the Book of Genesis, or from one of the Gospels, or from Proverbs. Maybe you could read some of your favorite Bible stories. From time to time on other days, add to your recording. Maybe you could listen to your tape while you go to sleep. Remember as you listen that it is *God* who is speaking to you in the Bible.

MONTH 3

Love God's Word

Jeremiah 36:20–26; Psalm 119:11

A. It would be good if, at some time, you would read all of Jeremiah 36. Do you know what a **scroll** is? A scroll is a long strip of paper with writing on it. The paper is usually rolled onto a stick at each end. The scroll you read about contained words that God gave to the prophet Jeremiah. A man named Baruch wrote these words down. The words were warnings from God to His people. Do you see what the king did to the scroll? Read verse 23 again. Think about how awful a thing that was to do. It is because the wicked king hated the words of God. He did not want to obey them. You should never be like that. We hope you will always love and honor God's Word. We hope you will be like the man who wrote the psalm you read. He loved God's Word so much that he hid it in his heart to help keep him from sinning. We hope you will do the same thing.

Underline the one who loved God's Word; circle the one who hated it:

a. the king   **b. the psalmist**

47

B. Every time you memorize a new verse of Scripture, write it down on an index card. Draw a picture or decorate each card. Keep the cards in a file box or small photo album. You will enjoy collecting these cards. We hope that they will help you to love God's Word better.

Praying

We have been learning that our Heavenly Father created all things, inspired the Bible, and sent His Son, the Lord Jesus to be our Savior. Isn't He great and wonderful? And do you know what else? We can talk to Him. We talk to Him by praying to Him. We hope that you talk to the Lord very often. If you belong to Jesus, your Heavenly Father *wants* you to pray. He even commands it. He wants us to praise Him, thank Him, tell Him things and ask Him for things. He wants us to come to Him in Jesus' Name. No one shines for Jesus without praying. We can pray at church, where God's people pray together. We can also pray with our families at family worship. And always, always we can pray when we are alone. In fact, you can pray wherever you are and whenever you want to. Isn't that a good thing to know?

When You Pray

If you do not know the Lord's Prayer, now is a good time to learn it. It is found in Matthew 6:9–13. When Jesus was teaching His disciples how to pray, He gave this prayer as a pattern.

Devotionals for Each Month

1. We Must Not Stop Praying
2. We Can Ask God for Things
3. Pray for Others

MONTH 1

We Must Not Stop Praying

Daniel 6:4–13

A. Do you know who Daniel was? He was a man who loved God very much. You probably already know this story, but if you do not, read all of this chapter in the Bible and talk to someone who can tell you more about it. Even though Daniel had to go to another country where the people did not know the true God, he knew how important prayer was. He kept on praying every day even though the king of the country had made a law that said he should not. Then, because Daniel disobeyed the king, wicked men told on him and he was thrown into the den of lions. Can you finish the story? The important thing for you to think about today is that you should want to be like Daniel. God has told you in His Word that you should pray. No one should be able to stop you from obeying Him.

Write true or false:
Daniel did right to disobey the king. _____

B. Take a little quiet time later. Play the "imagine" game. Close your eyes tight and pretend. Pretend your family had to move to another country. Maybe it would be as missionaries. Perhaps you have a magazine or letters at your house that tell about how hard it is for Christians in other countries. Pick one of those countries and imagine what it would be like if you had to live there. Pretend in your mind that you find out that there is a law that says no one is to pray to the Christian God or they will be punished. Can they stop you from praying? Would you obey that law?

MONTH 2

We Can Ask God for Things

2 Kings 19:14–19

A. Hezekiah was a good king. He was one of the best kings God's people ever had. But at this time he was in big trouble. You see, a wicked king who had a big and strong army wanted to fight King Hezekiah in a war. This wicked king sent a very mean letter to Hezekiah. The letter said mean things about God. This wicked king even said in his letter that God could not save King Hezekiah. Hezekiah did the best thing he could have done. He took his problem to the Lord Himself and asked for God's help. The Lord heard him and helped him. God scared away the wicked king and that king did not bother Hezekiah anymore. When we pray to God, we should always thank Him for our blessings. We talked about that on another day last month. Another thing we can do when we pray is to ask God for things. We can ask Him for help and ask Him for things we need. He will hear us and will answer in a way that is best for us.

What did Hezekiah do with the letter he received? (Circle the right answer).

a. burned it   b. showed it to God to read

B. Write a letter to God and ask Him for something. If you have a problem, ask for His help. Read your letter to God when you have your prayer time. Remember: God will always answer us in a way that is best for us.

MONTH 3

Pray for Others

Numbers 14:11–20

A. God had promised His people the land of Canaan. Their great leader Moses had sent twelve men to spy out the promised land. Ten of the men were afraid to go into the land to capture it. Two of the men trusted that God would keep His promise. These two men wanted to go in and take the land because they knew that the Lord would be with them. The people listened to the ten men who were afraid. God was very angry with the people. He was ready to take His blessings away from His people and give these blessings only to Moses. Moses was a humble man and did not want this, so he prayed to God on behalf of the people. He asked God to forgive them and God did. We should all be like Moses. We should pray for others. Even if others have done wrong we should pray for them. We hope that Moses will be a good example for you.

What did Moses do? (Circle the right answer)

a. prayed for the people
b. started being proud of himself

B. Here is something to do a little later: Pick someone special to pray for. It could be your pastor or a missionary or one of the leaders of your town or state or country. Or maybe it could be someone who is sick or in trouble. Draw a picture of that person on a four-by-six index card. Tape the card in a place where you will see it often. Whenever you look at the card, say a prayer for that person.

Loving Others

Who should you love best of all? God says that we must love *Him* more than anyone else. Who should you love next best? Should it be yourself? NO, NO, NO. God says that we should love others just as much as we love ourselves. That is very hard to do, isn't it? This is hard for all people to do, but especially for children, since children often think of themselves first. When that happens, these children do not look like the jewels we have been talking about. Loving others does not just have to do with the way we feel about others. It has more to do with the way we *treat* others. You will see that many of the things we talk about in this book have to do with ways to show our love for others and not to think of ourselves first. Children who are precious jewels that shine will love others and show it.

When You Pray

Pray and thank God for His love in Jesus. Ask Him to give you more love for others, even when it is hard.

Devotionals for Each Month

1. God's Law Teaches Us to Love Others
2. When We Love Others, We are Like Jesus
3. We Love Others by Serving

MONTH 1

God's Law Teaches Us to Love Others

Matthew 22:35–40

A. You probably know all about the Ten Commandments. Long ago, God gave these rules to His people to help them know how He wants them to live. The Ten Commandments are also called God's **Law**. The most important thing that we learn from God's Law is how to love and worship Him. That is what we learn from the first four commandments. The other very important thing that we learn in the last six commandments is how to love others. So you see, God not only wants us to love others, He also gives us many guidelines on how to do this. In your Bible reading, you saw that Jesus tells us that we should love other people as much as we love ourselves. It is very important that we all remember this, even children like you. All throughout this book you will be learning many ways that God wants you to show your love to your family, friends and other people.

Circle the right answer:

Jesus calls these other people your (cousins / neighbors).

B. Cut three four-by-six index cards in half. Then you will have six smaller cards. Write the numbers for the last six commandments on the six cards, starting with number five and ending with number ten. You should write one of those numbers on each of the six small cards. Put the cards in a brown paper bag. Have your dad or mom pick one of the cards out of the bag without you seeing it. Tell them to pretend they are disobeying that commandment and to let you guess which one it is. (They may need someone else to help them.) Then ask them to talk to you about how you can show love to others by *obeying* that commandment.

MONTH 2

When We Love Others, We Are Like Jesus

Ephesians 4:31–5:2

A. Do you know what it means to **imitate** someone? It means we try to do what that person does or to act like that person acts. If we love others, we are being like Jesus. We imitate Him. He loved us and gave Himself for us. If you love Jesus, you must love others as He did. Can you think of ways a child like you can show love? As we said before, many of the other devotionals we have been doing together are all about loving others. It is not just something we *feel*, it is something that we *do*. Show your love by being kind to your brothers and sisters and friends. Show your love by helping your dad and mom and others. Show your love by sharing with them and by giving to them. You can think of many ways, just like Jesus did.

Is this true?:

If we love others, we are following Jesus. _____

B. Get a parent's permission to play "Follow the Leader" later. When you are the leader, make your followers do some things that are easy and other things that are hard. Think about this: When we follow Jesus by loving others, is it always easy? Was it always easy for Jesus? If it is sometimes hard to love someone, should we show love to them anyway?

MONTH 3

We Love Others by Serving

John 13:3-5, 12-15

A. How often do you say "Me first" when you play a game or something good is being given out? Hopefully you don't say that too often. It is so much better to put others first. Don't you think that a person who serves another is putting that other person first? Jesus washed the feet of His friends. He was not thinking first of Himself. One reason He did this was to show that those who love Him should be servants to each other. He was showing His followers that He was willing to serve others and that we should be willing to do the same. You have many chances to serve in your home. Maybe sometimes you help a little brother or sister to put on their shoes or zip up their coat. That is a nice way to serve them. Serve your parents by doing something for them when they are tired, such as going and finding the book they are looking for or finding their pair of glasses for them or even helping them with their slippers. Just see how nice you will feel when you make others happy this way!

Circle the right answer:

Jesus followers must try to (serve others / be first).

63

B. On a piece of notebook paper, make a list of ways a child can serve others. Pick three things from your list and do them today. After that, try to make it a habit of doing at least one of those things every day without being asked. Show your list to your parents. They may have some suggestions for you.

Having Self-Control

Now, on this seventh day of the month, we will talk about **self-control**. Here is what we mean by self-control: Do you ever have to do something even when you do not feel like it—like sitting still in church or family worship? Do you ever wish you could tell someone something, but you know you should not tell it for one reason or another—so you don't say it? That is what we mean. Sometimes we feel something inside of us that makes us want to do something, but we know that what we feel is not the best thing at that time. Or, maybe we know something is best and we have bad feelings inside of us that make us not want to do it. These are all feelings that need to be controlled. In other words, we need to do what is right, even when our feelings would make us want to do otherwise. We need Jesus to help us to have control over our feelings and to do what pleases Him.

When You Pray

Ask God that these lessons will help you see that you cannot let your feelings be in control.

Devotionals for Each Month

1. Self-Control Helps Us Fight Satan
2. Esther Had Self-Control
3. Cain Did Not Have Self-Control

MONTH 1

Self-Control Helps Us Fight Satan

Proverbs 25:28

A. God has an enemy whose name is Satan. Satan is a very bad and wicked angel who hates God with all his might. Satan does not want to see anyone live for God. In fact, he tries to get people to do evil. That means he is *your* enemy, too. We must ask God the Holy Spirit to help us not to do what Satan wants us to do. If we do not ask God to help us to **rule over**, or **control** our spirits (feelings), it will be easier for Satan to make us do wrong. Then we would be like a city whose walls have come down so that the enemies of that city can get in. Don't let your enemy, Satan, stop you from doing what's right. Ask God the Holy Spirit to help you control any feelings which are not pleasing to Him, so that you might be protected from this wicked enemy. Do you think self-control could keep you from telling a lie, or saying something mean, or from pouting when you should be cheerfully obeying? These are all things that Satan would like to see you do. How many other things can you think of?

Circle the right word:

The Holy Spirit will help us to
(rule over / live with) our own spirits.

B. Here is something to do today: Pick a small stuffed animal or beanie. Put a blanket or sheet on the floor to keep everything clean. Now, build a wall around your little friend: use pillows or rolled towels or boxes or whatever you can think of to make your wall (make sure what you use is okay with your dad or mom). After a short time, knock down your wall. If this had been a real wall, when was your little friend safer—before or after the wall was knocked down? Why? According to your lesson today, when are *you* safer?

MONTH 2

Esther Had Self-Control

Esther 4:10–17

A. Queen Esther was very afraid. She did not want to go in to see her husband, the king. She could be killed if she did that without being called. But her cousin Mordecai had sent her a very sad message: her people, the Jews, were all going to be killed and only the king could help them. Esther knew she needed to try to help her people. What if the king was angry that she came in to talk to him? But she had to do it, even though he could have her killed. She had to do it, because it was the right thing to do. She had to try to help her people. And do you know what? She *did* go in to the king, and God protected her—and her people! So Esther did what she knew was right even though she did not feel like doing it. Esther had self-control.

Write True or False:
Esther went in to see the king because she wanted to.

_____

B. Maybe when you have your family devotions, you could learn more about the Book of Esther. Ask these questions: How did Esther become queen? Did the king know she was a Jew? Who was Haman? Who was Mordecai? Why did Haman hate Mordecai? Why did the king make the law to have the Jews killed? Now, these questions are for you: Did you like the way the story ended? Did Esther want to go see the king? Why did she do it? Was this good control of her feelings? Is there anything that you read today in the Bible that lets you know that she probably prayed first? Is there something that you need to do and you don't feel like doing it? Who can help you to do it anyway?

MONTH 3

Cain Did Not Have Self-Control

Genesis 4:1–8

A. Today we will talk about anger. Anger is a feeling that we can have against another person. If we do not control it, it can be very bad and lead to very bad things. Cain started out by being angry with his brother Abel. Then, he began to hate Abel. If anger is not controlled, often it becomes hatred. Cain's hatred became so strong that he ended up killing his brother. The sixth commandment teaches us that we are not to kill another person. You may think that you have never broken that commandment. But did you know Jesus said that if we have angry and hateful feelings about someone else, we have broken the sixth commandment? It is very, very important that we control our anger. Sometimes a brother or sister or friend will receive something you think you should have gotten. Maybe someone was praised for doing something and nobody said anything about you. Be very careful that you do not let anger creep into your heart about this and that you do not begin to resent the other person. Pray for God's help. Here is another verse for you: 1 John 3:15. Remember it.

Yes or No:

Cain broke the sixth commandment when he did not control his anger. _____

B. Get a grown-up to help you do this: Put a tablespoon of baking soda into a small bowl. Set the bowl in a sink. Then slowly add some vinegar or lemon juice to it. Do you see the bubbles forming? Does it run over the edge of the bowl? Do you know that if you have anger inside of you and you let it stay there, you could end up with bad "bubbles" in you? They can "spill over" and cause you to think and say and do bad things. Anger can make you think wicked thoughts and it can even make you do wicked things. You do not want anger to bubble up inside. If it comes, ask God to take it away.

Obeying Your Parents

One day, you might want to sit down and write all of the Ten Commandments in order without looking. Do you think you could do that? Even if you cannot, it is probably a good time to begin to learn them. We hope that you love these commandments and try with all your heart to obey them all. You may know one of them very well—that would be the fifth commandment. You probably have heard how important this commandment is to children. That is because it teaches you that you should love and honor your parents, as well as all others whom God puts over you. In each of these three devotionals, we are going to try to help you to remember how important it is to be an obedient child. If you do love and honor your parents, you will obey them. To be **obedient** means to do what you are told to do. If you are obedient, you will quickly and cheerfully do as you are told. You will do this with a heart of trust. If you obey the Bible's command to honor your parents, you will have many blessings from God. And surely you know that obedient children are the ones whom Jesus would call jewels.

When You Pray

Memorize Exodus 20:12 and pray that the Lord will help you to always keep this commandment.

Devotionals for Each Month

1. God Made Parents Rulers
2. Parents Must Teach Their Children
3. Jesus Obeyed His Parents

MONTH 1

God Made Parents Rulers

Colossians 3:20; Proverbs 6:20–22

A. Do you know what it means when someone rules? It means that person decides what should or should not be done. A king rules his kingdom. A judge rules in a court. Teachers rule in a classroom. God made it so that parents, especially fathers, rule in the home. *God* is the One who says that you should honor your father and mother. He wants children to do this by loving, helping, and obeying their parents. Of course, this means *you*, too. What a blessing God has given to you if you have parents who love and care about your soul. Be thankful for them and show your thankfulness by your obedience. And don't forget: not only do they rule over you, but they protect you, too.

Write True or False:
If children obey their parents, they are obeying God.

———————

B. Set up a chair in the living room or family room. You might want to wrap it with ribbons or tie on balloons.

Tell everyone this is your "throne" and you are king (or queen). Tell your family that everyone has to do what you say when you sit on your throne. Do they all obey you when you rule? Who made you king or queen? *Should* they obey you? Who made your parents to rule in your home? Why should you obey them?

MONTH 2

Parents Must Teach Their Children

1 Samuel 2:12; 3:10–13; 4:10–11

A. Once there was a priest named Eli. It is very sad, but this good man had two very wicked sons. We do not know for sure, but it is possible they turned out to be so wicked because their father had not made them obey when they were little. We do know that when they did become grown men and did many bad things, their father Eli did not honor God enough to make them stop. These two sons brought shame to God's people and were both killed the same day as God's punishment to them and their father. Be thankful for parents who teach you to obey. When they do, they are honoring God. If you have a father who is making sure that you follow the fifth commandment, you have a wonderful blessing. It is very possible that this could help you not to grow up to be wicked like Eli's sons.

Write True or False:
The Lord did not blame Eli for his sons' bad behavior.

_____

B. The Bible tells us that Eli's sons did not know the Lord (1 Samuel 2:12). Parents are to teach their children what it means to know and love Jesus. He is the One who will help you to want to be obedient. Make up a list of questions to ask your parents about how they came to be Christians. Pretend you are doing an **interview** and read the questions to them. Then ask them questions about how *you* can come to know Jesus. Pray that the Savior will work in your heart as you learn from your dad and mom and pastors and teachers.

*(**Note:** An interview is what they call it when someone meets with another person to talk to them and ask them questions about something.)*

MONTH 3

Jesus Obeyed His Parents

Luke 2:40–52

A. Remember that we learned that Jesus is God's Son? He Himself is God. We call Him God the Son. Does God have to obey anyone? Even though Jesus came down to earth as a little baby who grew to be a little boy, and then grew even more to become a man, He was always still God. The Bible passage you just read tells us that even though He was the Son of God, Jesus was **subject** to His earthly parents. That means that He obeyed them; He did what they told Him to do with a willing heart. He did this because it was right. He did this because it would have been sinful if He had not. And Jesus *never* sinned. Also, Jesus was showing us that He wants all of His children to obey their parents. You are being like Jesus when you obey.

Fill in the word:

If children are to be like Jesus, they must _____ their parents.

79

B. Later, use your chalkboard or dry-erase board: Draw a picture of your family. Circle the people in the picture you should be subject to. Show the picture to your parents. Tell them you read that Jesus was subject to His parents and that you should be, too.

Being Kind

Are you a kind person? Are you a person who cares about others? Do you care about how what you say or do makes others feel? If you make another person sad, does that make you sad? Does it please you to make others feel better or to make them happy? If you answered "yes" to these questions, then you are probably a kind person. **Kindness** will keep you from falling into many of the sins that children are known for. It will keep you from teasing other children about things that will make them feel sad about themselves. It will keep you from laughing at them or whispering about them. If you know someone who has problems, kindness will help you to go to that person and see what you can do to help. There are many children who are not kind. We certainly hope that you are not one of them. Children who are not kind do not make pretty, sparkling gems.

When You Pray

Here is a good prayer for you: "Lord help me always to do and say kind things, to obey You and be kind, and may the Holy Spirit help me to grow the fruit of kindness. Amen."

Devotionals for Each Month

1. We Can See and Hear Kindness
2. God Commands Us to be Kind
3. Kindness is a Fruit of the Spirit

MONTH 1

We Can See and Hear Kindness

2 Samuel 9:1–8

A. When we talk about being kind to someone, we should **see** our kindness in the way we treat that person or **hear** it in the way we talk to them. In your Bible reading, did you see and hear King David's kindness to King Saul's grandson? Did you "hear" how gentle King David was when he talked to the young man? Did you "see" what David was doing for him—giving him his grandfather's land and letting him eat at David's table like he was a part of the family? You can be kind like David was. You can speak sweet and gentle words and do kind and helpful things for others.

Fill in the words: (Pick from the list.)

Kindness is something we can _____ and _____.

[Word List: eat, hear, sleep, read, see]

B. Maybe you know someone who does not see or hear very well. It could be someone older, like a grandparent or great-grandparent or a person in a nursing home. Maybe you know someone with a **handicap**. This means that something in that person's body does not work very well. The man in the Bible story had lame feet, so he had a handicap. His feet did not work as they should. If you do know people who cannot see, hear, or walk well or something else, we want you to think of ways that you can let them see or hear kindness from you. What can you do or say to help them? You can do something, you know, even as young as you are. Ask your parents to help you think of what you can do. By the way, if *you* are a child who has a handicap, we want you to know that your Father in Heaven knows all about you, and that He cares about you and loves you just as you are. You will see and hear kindness from Him in His Word and through others who love you.

MONTH 2

God Commands Us to Be Kind

Ephesians 4:31–32

A. On another day we will talk about anger. Anger is something that makes us feel mean and talk mean. It is much more pleasant to talk about being kind, isn't it? We do not want to forget about how important kindness is. God has commanded that we show kindness to each other—He wants us to be nice to one another. He wants us to be forgiving if someone wrongs us. There may be a few people you have a little trouble being kind to. Let's just say you have a little brother or sister who does things that are upsetting to you. You would not push them roughly out of your way or shout at them, would you? Can you still act kindly and talk nicely to them, anyway? You must, you know. God has told you to be kind to others. You need to obey Him. As with everything else He commands you to do, if you ask Him to help you to be kind, He will.

Circle the answer:

To obey God, we must try to be:
a. smarter than others   **b. kind to others**

B. Here is what you can do today: Take your dry-erase board or chalkboard and draw a line down the middle. Then, on the left side, draw a happy face for each time you say or do something nice today. Now, if you will be brave and honest, draw a sad face on the other side each time you are unkind. Remember these faces and pray about them when you go to bed. Even after you stop using this "chart," think about what you did today and try to obey the Lord with lots of happy faces.

MONTH 3

Kindness is a Fruit of the Spirit

Galatians 5:22–23

A. Our Father in Heaven knows how hard it is for us to always do right. That is why Jesus has sent the Holy Spirit to live in us and help us to be good. In your Bible reading, you learned about the kind of fruit that God's children should bear (or grow). Good apples grow on good apple trees and good pears grow on good pear trees. But the kind of fruit the Bible is talking about is all the good things that God's children do and think. It is fruit that grows in our hearts. The Holy Spirit lives in the heart of each person who loves and belongs to Jesus. It is God the Holy Spirit who helps good fruit to grow in our hearts. Kindness is one of the good fruit that the Holy Spirit helps us to have. So you must pray for help from God to be kind.

Write True or False:

Because we have good hearts already, it is easy for us to be kind. _____

B. During snack or lunch, eat a piece of fruit. Choose fruit that has seeds in it, like an apple or orange or watermelon. Take out a seed and look at it. Isn't it wonderful how our Creator, God, gave each fruit its own kind of seed? Did you know that more of that fruit, even a tree for that kind of fruit, could grow from that seed? Who or what needs to be in your heart if you are to grow the fruit of kindness? While you eat your piece of fruit today and whenever you eat this fruit again, think about whether or not you have the fruit of God's Spirit, especially kindness.

Watching Your Tongue

In Psalm 141:3, we read the words, "Set a guard, O Lord, over my mouth, keep watch over the door of my lips." Do you know what this means? When you **guard** something, it means you watch over it. You want to keep it safe and protect it. Sometimes to guard something means you carefully watch over it to keep it from getting away. This verse is a prayer we all should pray. It asks God to help us to be careful of what we say. We need Him to guard, or watch over, the way we talk. The way we use our tongues is important to God. In the second chapter of the Book of James in the Bible, we read some other things about our tongues. We read how hard it is to tame the tongue. When something is **tame** it is not wild; it is controlled. Do not forget how God feels about this—we should try our best to glorify Him with our words.

When You Pray

Pray the prayer in Psalm 141:3 and ask that the Lord will do this for you. Also memorize these two verses and pray that you will be given help to live by them: Proverbs 10:19 and James 1:19.

Devotionals for Each Month

1. Our Words Can Help
2. Our Words Can Hurt
3. The Third Commandment

MONTH 1

Our Words Can Help

Proverbs 16:24

A. Yesterday we talked about how we can see kindness and how we can hear it. We said that when we are kind, we can hear it in the words we say. When something is **pleasant** it means it is nice; it makes people feel happier. Our words can be pleasant. When they are, the Bible says they make the other person feel "sweet" inside. That means they feel better. If a person is sad or sick, your pleasant words can help them. Sometimes your words will make them feel happy again or, at least, cheer them up a little. Older people who are lonely and do not feel well often can feel better by the words of children. Your kind and gentle talking or your cheerful and happy conversation could mean more to these people than you might think. Who is there that needs you to say kind, sweet things to them? If you try hard enough, you will think of someone.

Circle the right answer:
Our nice words are like (lemons / honey).

B. Pleasant words make us feel better, like medicine does. Sometimes people mix lemon juice and honey together to make medicine for a cold. Have you ever had it? It really does help when you have a bad cough. Try tasting some honey and some lemon juice when they are not mixed together: Ask if you can get two little plastic cups. Put lemon juice in one and honey in the other. Taste each one, with sips of water in between. Which taste do you like better? Which taste is more pleasant? Are sweet things usually more pleasant to you than sour or bitter things? They are for most people. Do you say words that are sweet most of the time rather than sour or bitter words? Do your words help people to feel better?

MONTH 2

Our Words Can Hurt

1 Samuel 1:1−7

A. You probably know about this story. There was a man who had two wives—one named Peninnah, who had several children, and one named Hannah, who had no children. Many of us know about Hannah's prayer and we know that God did one day give her a son in answer to her prayer. But before that, Hannah was very sad and cried a lot. Yes, she was sad that she had no children. She wanted children very much. But do you know what made her even sadder, and why she cried and cried and sometimes could not eat? It was because the other wife made fun of her and teased her about it. These words hurt Hannah very much.

You should never do this. You should never say things to another person that will make him feel bad about himself. You should at least try to think about whether what you say will make someone else hurt more. Suppose you are good at playing sports and you know someone who is not good at sports. Would you tease that person because he can't hit the ball, or run fast, or catch? How would the Lord feel about it if you did? There are many other things you could tease others about that would make them feel bad. Never, never do that.

93

Write in the answer:

Did the other wife's words make Hannah feel better or worse? _____

B. This is a good time to get out some puppets. It would be fun to make a couple of them out of socks and fix them up to look like ladies. Even paper bags would do. Anyway, take two puppets and make them talk to each other. One can be Peninnah and the other Hannah. Make the Peninnah puppet say some of the things that Peninnah probably said to Hannah. Did you make her say words that hurt Hannah? Now, make the Peninnah puppet say things that would be right to say to another person who has a problem. We hope this will be a lesson to you about the kind of things you should <u>not</u> say to other people.

MONTH 3

The Third Commandment

Exodus 20:7

A. You have just read the third commandment. The third commandment has a lot to do with watching our tongues. Among other things, it has to do with how we use God's name. It teaches that we should not be careless with the holy name of God. We should talk about God and His Word and His works in a high and holy way. We should not repeat jokes about God or His ways. We should not use His name in a careless way, such as when we say "Oh, my God" or "Oh, Lord" when we are not even thinking about Him. Of course, we know that we should not use bad language (swear words and curse words), but it is also wrong to say God's name in ways that do not honor Him. Rather, we should only say His name in ways that show our respect and love for Him. And don't forget, the way we live must show that we honor His name.

Fill in the blank:
We should be very careful how we use God's

_____

B. Have some fun with nicknames today. Do you know what a **nickname** is? It is something we call a person or thing in place of their real name—like "Jimmy" instead of "James." Some nicknames are funny. Make a list of the people you know who are called by nicknames instead of their real names. Put their nicknames down next to their real names. If you can, talk to some of them and ask them if they like their nicknames. Now, think about this: Should we ever give God a nickname? Why or why not? When you talk to people about their nicknames, explain to them what you learned today about the use of God's name.

Being a Helper

One of the best ways that children can shine is by being helpers. You will be such a blessing to others if you have a willing, helpful spirit. This is especially true in your home with your family. Even when you were a toddler, you helped your daddy and mommy. You could pick up things and go get things for them. Now that you are growing older, you can *really* be a good helper. You can do so many things to be a help at home, at school, at church, or even when visiting at someone else's home. Not only will you be serving others, but you will be serving Jesus, as well.

When You Pray

Pray that the Lord will start working in your heart so that you will want to be a helper. Then pray that He will show you ways you can be helpful wherever you are.

Devotionals for Each Month

1. We Help When We Obey
2. We Help in Little Ways
3. We Must Be Happy Helpers

MONTH 1

We Help When We Obey

1 Samuel 15:17–23

A. If you are given a job to do or if you are helping your parents, teachers or anyone else whom God has put over you, you must do what you are told to do. When you do not do what you are told to do and do not follow the commands you are given, then you are not really helping. A good helper is an obedient one.

King Saul was given a job to do by God. He thought he could do the job his way, not God's way. Later, God took Saul's kingdom from him because he did not obey. Let's suppose your Sunday school teacher asks you to put away the pencils after your lesson. Suppose you decide to put the pencils in a different place than where you were told to put them, because you think they would be better in the place you picked. Is that really being a good helper? If you were to *really* help, don't you think it would be best to do exactly what you were told to do? Shouldn't your teacher know that you will follow the commands just as they were given? This is true whenever you help someone else. You should be the kind of helper who listens carefully and then does what is expected.

Write the correct letter:

God was angry with Saul for _____.
a. killing the Amalekites   **b. not obeying**

B. Do a stick puppet play about 1 Samuel 15:1–23. Draw your puppet players on construction paper with colored pencils and then cut them out. Draw Samuel, Saul, King Agag, a few Amalekites and some sheep and oxen. Glue your puppets on Popsicle sticks or straws. In your play, show what Samuel told Saul to do. Then show what Saul did. Then show what Samuel said to Saul. Do your play during family time and explain to everyone what kind of helper Saul was and what kind of helper you should be.

MONTH 2

We Help in Little Ways

John 6:5–14

A. We are almost certain that you have heard this story many times—Jesus fed 5,000 people with five loaves of bread and two little fish! Nobody but God could do such a thing! Now, what we want you to think about is where Jesus got this food to feed all those people. That's right, a young boy shared his lunch with Jesus. Look at the big thing that happened after this boy helped in such a small way. Just think, you could also do just a *little* something to help someone. You are not too young, you know. And if you did, who knows how God could use even that. Do you think maybe there are little things you can help Mother with in the kitchen? Folding socks or emptying wastebaskets may seem like small things, but it is a big help to your parents. Fetching things and bringing them to a parent or grandparent may seem small, but it could be a very *big* help to them. What other things can you think of? Whatever you do, no matter how small, the Lord might use it in somebody else's life.

Write True or False:

We do not need to do big things to help Jesus.

_____

B. Make five little loaves of bread and two fish out of playdough. Put these in a basket. Pretend you are feeding them to a huge number of people. Could _you_ do that? Could Jesus do that if you gave what you had to Him like the boy did? Of course, the answer to the second question is "yes." There are many little things you can give to Jesus to help Him: You can be a good helper to your parents, sisters and brothers, teachers and friends. Jesus can use all of the little things you might do for them.

MONTH 3

We Must Be Happy Helpers

Psalm 100

A. Do you see what verse two says? We should serve the Lord with **gladness**. This means that when we help others, we should do that with gladness, also. If you do something for another person and you are grumpy about it, you are not really helping them as much as when you do it with a cheerful and happy spirit. Knowing that you are helping that person should give you a happy and contented heart. Some of your happiness will rub off on the one you are helping, so then don't you think everyone will be happier?

Are you a happy helper? Do others see a happy face or a grouchy face when you are helping them? What kind of face does Jesus want to see?

Write in the correct word:

We should serve others _____.
a. sadly   b. gladly

B. On a white paper plate, draw a big smiley face. You will probably want to use your colored pencils to draw hair and to color the smiley face. Now, write the words to the first part of Psalm 100:2 on the plate.

Put tape on the back and put the paper plate up on the wall or door of the kitchen or family room or some other place where you will see it a lot. It will remind you to be a happy helper around your home.

Working Hard

Some people think that children spend most of their time playing, and maybe that is true of many children. But God's children should have work to do. Work is good for us. Hard workers grow stronger and they are often happier. Not only does work make our bodies stronger, but it makes our minds healthier. There are many different kinds of work that we must do. There is schoolwork, housework, yard work, and other types of work. As you grow older, you will be spending more and more hours of the day doing work. Do you have chores that you must do every day? If so, good. Eat healthy foods and get plenty of sleep at night so that you can work hard and do your work well. On another day, we will talk about doing your best. Today, we will talk about working *hard.* The jobs that you have to do will not always be easy, but hang in there and get them done. Hard work makes Jesus' jewels sparkle. You do not want to be dull and lazy. You want to be sparkling and ready to work.

When You Pray

"Dear Lord, thank you for all the fun times I get to have. Help me to be thankful, too, that I have work to do. Help me to be a hard worker. Amen."

Devotionals for Each Month

1. God Helps Us Do Hard Work
2. The Eighth Commandment
3. Do Not Be Lazy

MONTH 1

God Helps Us Do Hard Work

Nehemiah 2:1–6; 4:6

A. Nehemiah was one of God's people. He was very sad. He was sad because of what he had heard about God's city of Jerusalem. The walls of the city were broken down and the gates burned with fire. Nehemiah was a servant of the King of Persia. One day, the king noticed that Nehemiah was sad and asked him why. Nehemiah was brave enough to tell the king about God's city and after praying for God's help, he asked the king to let him go to Jerusalem to lead the people in rebuilding the city. God touched the king's heart and he let Nehemiah go! So Nehemiah went to do this hard work and God helped him. There were enemies who mocked Nehemiah and the people who worked with him. There were even dangers from swords and arrows. God gave Nehemiah the strength to lead the people, and the hard work of building the walls and gates of the city was finished. God helped Nehemiah to do this hard work. Don't you think He will do the same for you if you have hard work to do?

B. There are probably things that are hard for you to do, like cleaning your room. Maybe doing arithmetic is hard for you, or learning to read and write. Some children think it is hard to memorize Bible verses. Get a chalkboard or dry-erase board. Draw a picture of you doing the thing that is hardest for you to do. Pray and ask God for His help in doing this hard work and ask others to pray for you, too.

MONTH 2

The Eighth
Commandment

Exodus 20:15; Ephesians 4:28

A. The eighth commandment teaches us something we must never forget: we should not take anything that belongs to someone else without their permission. It teaches us that we should do our own work. If we do our work well, God will bless us with what we need. If we ask God to help us to be good workers and to be content, we will not be as tempted to steal. Cheating is also a type of stealing. If we cheat on our schoolwork or in a game, we are taking something that does not belong to us. We must do our own work and trust God to provide. We can steal many things. Of course, we know that we can steal money and another's possessions, but did you know that you can also steal time? Have you ever heard of the word "dawdle"? When someone **dawdles**, he takes too long to do whatever he is doing. He takes more time than is necessary. This could happen when someone is eating breakfast or getting dressed in the morning or doing chores and schoolwork. For the most part, if that person is not sick or handicapped in some way, he is wasting time. This can become a very bad habit and when it does, that person is stealing time that really does not belong to him. Remember this when you are doing your hard work.

Circle the best answer:

Work is good for us. It helps to keep us from:
a. getting tired.   b. taking what is not ours.

B. Here is a way to earn twenty-five or fifty cents: Ask one of your parents to give you a special job to do. Maybe you could help clean a certain room or closet or something else. Ask your dad or mom to hide five nickels or five dimes (let them decide which) in secret places so that you can find the money as you work. That will be your pay. Isn't it a good feeling to get money by working? You and your parents can think of other ways you can earn money. We hope that when you grow up you will be a good worker and that you will never get anything the wrong way.

MONTH 3

Do Not Be Lazy

Proverbs 6:6–11

A. In the passage you just read, you can see that the Lord is not pleased with the person He calls a "sluggard." A **sluggard** is a person who does not want to work. We call that person lazy. God is telling the lazy person to look at how the ants work. He says that lazy people can learn from ants, because ants are hard workers. God also says that those who are lazy often like to sleep too much and will end up being poor when they don't have to be. He is not saying that if you are poor it always means you are lazy, but He is saying that laziness often does cause poverty. Your parents will give you work to do because they care about what kind of person you will grow up to be. They do not want you to be the kind of person God is talking about in these verses.

Fill in the word:

A sluggard is a _____ person.

B. During your reading time today, we hope that you can read or that someone will read to you *The Ant and the Grasshopper*, which is one of Aesop's Fables. After you

111

read this, think hard about what is happening in this story. You can see that this is a story about two different kinds of insects. After reading about them, which insect do you want to be like? The next time you feel lazy when there is work to do, remember this story. If being lazy becomes a habit, you could end up like the grasshopper in the story. Listen carefully to what God is teaching you about this in His Word.

Trusting God

When you **trust** someone, it means that you know that you can depend on that person. When you trust people, you are sure they will not harm you on purpose. It also means that you believe what they say and you believe that they will do what they feel is best for you. You have faith and confidence in people you trust. Children can trust their parents. The One we can trust more than anyone else is our Father in Heaven. We can trust God at all times and in all things. Are you trusting God? On this thirteenth day of the month you will see some of the ways and times you can trust Him.

When You Pray

Let us pray: "It makes me very thankful to know that we can depend on you, dear Lord. Please help me to remember that you will always do what is best for me. Amen."

Devotionals for Each Month

1. Trusting God's Loving Care
2. Trusting God's Power and Greatness
3. Trusting God With Problems

MONTH 1

Trusting God's Loving Care

Matthew 6:25–34

A. This is one of the many beautiful lessons that Jesus taught His followers. It is such a wonderful lesson for boys and girls to learn, as well as their dads and moms. You see, Jesus is teaching all of us that our Father in Heaven knows our needs. He knows we need food to keep us strong and healthy, and clothes to keep our bodies warm. We can trust Him to give these things to us. After all, doesn't He give the birds and flowers what they need? What He wants is for *you* to not worry about what you are going to eat or wear, but to think most about pleasing and serving Him.

Circle the answer:

In verse 26, who has more value to God?
(the birds / us)

B. Perhaps this is something you could do today: If it is nice weather, go outside and see how many kinds of birds you see. If it is cold or rainy, sit and look for them out of your window. Write down the names of three of these birds. See if you can find out what these three kinds of birds eat—seeds or bugs or both (you could find this out in a book about birds or in a reference book). Where do they find their food? Do they ever buy it at the store? Do they cook it? Do you get your food at the store? Does it get cooked usually? Who gives food to the birds? Who gives food to you? Why should you not worry about being fed?

MONTH 2

Trusting God's Power and Greatness

1 Kings 17:1–16

A. Maybe you know about the prophet Elijah. He was a very great prophet of God. Maybe you know about how God sent Elijah to talk to the wicked King Ahab. God was not going to send any rain for a long time. This is called a **drought**. When there is a drought in a place, then there is a shortage of food, because wheat and corn and other things cannot grow. This is called a **famine**. Animals and people die from hunger. God sent this particular drought as a punishment because King Ahab had been leading the people to do evil. Now, do you see how God took care of His prophet during this famine? First, He sent him to a brook to live for a while. God sent birds called ravens to Elijah to bring him food, and he drank the water from the brook. After that, God fed Elijah and a widow woman for a long time, and all they had was a little flour along with a little oil in a jar. You can really see how powerful and great God is to do these things. You can see that He can do anything. Everything that is important to you is under His control. You can trust His power and greatness.

Circle the answers:

Who stopped the rain? (Elijah / God);
Who fed Elijah? (God / the widow)

B. See if your family can make popcorn later. Be a helper. Go get a big bowl and help put the popcorn into the bowl. Look at what happened to those little pieces of corn! Did your corn popper or microwave do a miracle? A **miracle** is something wonderful that happens which cannot be explained. It is an event that is not normal according to the laws of nature that God has established. We are just joking about the popcorn being a miracle. But those things that happened to Elijah really were miracles. Does this make you feel more safe and secure? Enjoy your popcorn and think about all this while you do.

MONTH 3

Trusting God with Problems

Luke 18:35–43

A. You just read about a man who sat by the side of a road begging for money. This man had a problem: he was blind. No one had been able to help him with this problem. But Jesus came along the road that day and the man knew that *Jesus* could help him. So he cried out to Jesus for mercy and Jesus heard him and helped him. Jesus helped this man with his problem by healing him. Now he could see! As we said on the sixteenth of last month, we all have problems from time to time. We are sure that you and your family have difficult things sometimes. This is the way it is with life. It is so good that we can trust God with our hard things. He may not always do exactly what we want, but we can trust Him that He *will* help us in a way that will work for our good.

Answer Yes or No:
Does God always heal people when they ask Him to?

_____

B. Later today, look up Psalm 34:15 in your Bible. This is a very good verse to remember. Write each word of the verse on a separate little piece of colorful paper. Write the words with markers. Glue the words in order on a piece of construction paper. Draw a border or add stickers or whatever you like. Now, take this verse and show it to your parents and ask them to explain its meaning to you. Ask them to explain who the **righteous** are in the verse. Think about yourself. Are *you* one of the righteous? If you are, what promise is God making to you? Hang up the verse in your room.

Telling the Truth

This is the day of the month that we will talk about being truthful. One of the sins that children often have trouble with is the sin of lying. Many times, children tell lies because they have done something wrong and they do not want to get into trouble for it. We hope that you do not do this. It is good if you always try to be honest, no matter what the situation is. To lie to your parents is one of the worst things that you can do. Make sure that they can always trust your word so that they can care for you as they should. Then they can help you to grow up to be a person who can be trusted and believed.

When You Pray

Seek the help of the Lord as you think about the need to be always truthful. Pray this way: "Dear Father in Heaven, please keep my heart and my lips from the sin of lying. Please help my parents and others to be able to trust what I do and say. Please help me to always tell the truth so that they will. In Jesus Name, Amen."

Devotionals for Each Month

1. Let Your Words Be Truthful
2. Let Your Actions Be Truthful
3. Sometimes We Should Keep the Truth to Ourselves

MONTH 1

Let Your Words Be Truthful

Exodus 20:16; Ephesians 4:25

A. You just read the ninth commandment in your Exodus reading. This and the verse in Ephesians teach us to speak the truth. This means that when we talk about something or someone, or if we tell something to another person, we should make sure we are careful to tell it right. We should not add things to what we are telling, and we should not leave out some of the facts, either. It is very easy to get into the habit of adding things and changing what is true, just a little bit. Be careful—you might want to change things a little to stay out of trouble or to make yourself look better. Then you stray away from the truth. It is also very wrong to say things about someone else when you are not sure what you are saying is correct. Please try not to say things to fool people on purpose. It is very easy to lie—again, be careful!

Is this true?:
It is all right to change the truth just a little bit.

_____

123

B. Read with a parent the story of *The Boy Who Cried Wolf,* an Aesop's Fable. What do you think of what the boy did? Was this a good way for him to have fun? Sometimes when we say things to tease other people, are we lying? Talk to your parents about some other ways that people can lie with their words. Remember to ask God to help you not to sin in any of these ways.

MONTH 2

Let Your Actions Be Truthful

Genesis 27:15–24

A. Have you ever heard the word "deceive"? When someone **deceives** another person, he tries to make that other person think things are different than they really are. Jacob did not only lie with his mouth but he lied to his father by his actions, too. He made his father think something that was not true. He deceived his father so that he could get his brother's blessing. Jacob's mother helped him to do this. This was very wrong for this wife and son to do, even though God was still ruling in it all, and God still was going to do His will. Hopefully, you will never be a person who deceives other people on purpose. Don't pretend you are sick if you are not, don't pretend you are busy if you are not, and don't ever try to use tears to get your own way. All these actions are deceitful and God will not be pleased. We hope that you want to please God in every way you can.

Write True or False:

The only way to lie is by saying something that is not true. _____

B. Play a trick on someone today. Do <u>not</u> do anything that could harm anybody, but only the kind of trick that people play on April 1st. *You* think of something. If you do something silly and tell the other person right away that you tricked him, he will probably laugh and think it is funny. But it is not funny to trick or deceive people and let them believe it. Make sure you tell the truth in what you say *and* do.

MONTH 3

Sometimes We Should Keep the Truth to Ourselves

Proverbs 11:12-13

A. Remember when we talked about watching your tongue and about how our words can hurt? For example, sometimes we can hurt others by mocking them or teasing them. But sometimes we can also hurt others if we simply say something about them that is true. If you tell about a matter knowing that what you tell will hurt someone, then it is wrong. Sometimes what you know about something does not need to be told. If that is so, it is best to keep it to yourself. It is not always needful to tell what someone else has done wrong. It is very important to pray to God for His wisdom to help you decide whether you should tell about something another person has done. Ask God to help you to decide if telling it will help or hurt that other person. If you think it will help them, go and tell it to your parents or pastor or someone whom you know you can trust. Don't gossip about it to others and don't be a tattletale who tries to get others in trouble. Whatever you do, do it with love in your heart.

Write True or False:

God always wants us to tell everything we know.

_____

B. During your reading time, read the poem "Two and One" in Appendix A. First read it silently and then read it to your mom or dad. Talk about what you think it means. Then read the second part of Ecclesiastes 3:7. Give some examples to your dad or mom of "a time to keep silent" and then of "a time to speak."

Being Responsible

To be **responsible** means you do what is expected of you. It means you can be depended upon to do what you are supposed to do. It means you do what you *should* do, even if it is not what you would *rather* do. If you would like to go outside and ride your bike, jump rope, play ball or some other fun thing, you will do your chores first or your schoolwork, or see to it that you have put away clutter before you go out. If you make this a habit, you are being responsible. You are really being a sparkling jewel!

When You Pray

> Pray that the Lord will help you to please Him every day by being a responsible child. Ask Him to help you to grow up to be a person others can count on to do what is expected of you.

Devotionals for Each Month

1. Do Your Duty
2. Keep Your Word
3. Take Care of Things

MONTH 1

Do Your Duty

Luke 17:10

A. All of us have **duties**. Once you know what your duty is, you need to get it done and try to do it right. This has a lot to do with obedience. Your parents and teachers will give you tasks or jobs to do. These are duties that you have. They are your **obligations**. You need to go ahead and do that work without having to be reminded over and over again. If you have certain jobs to do each week, you should not have to be told to do them each and every time. You should be responsible by going ahead and doing your chores and schoolwork even when you are not reminded. This will make your parents and teachers proud of you. But best of all, it will be pleasing to God and make you shine all the more for Him.

Circle the best answer:
**When we have chores to do, we (should / should not)
need to be reminded each time we do them.**

B. If you have grown-ups who say it is okay, and if you can get a group of childen together, play the game called "Contrary Children." This is how to play: The leader gives commands and everybody is supposed to do the opposite. Players who are caught doing what they are told, and not the opposite, must leave the game. The last player who is left wins. This game can be a lot of fun and it often makes children laugh. Is it funny in real life when children do not do what they are told to do? Will your parents and teachers laugh if you do not do your duty? What does Jesus think about that?

MONTH 2

Keep Your Word

Genesis 21:1–7

A. God had made a promise. He promised Abraham and Sarah, two older people, that He would give them a son. And He did. God did just what He said He would do. Do you see what verse 1 says? "The Lord did for Sarah as He had spoken." We know that the Lord can do anything. He keeps all His promises. We are not God, so there are many things we cannot do. But if we are to be responsible, we should only promise to do what we *can* do and once we say we are going to do a thing, we should do all in our power to do what we say. Do you ever promise friends that they can come over? It is not a good idea to make that promise without first checking to see if you really can have them over. And if you are able to have them and you promise them, then do all that you can to do it. Try to be this way about all of the promises you make.

Is this true?:

It is nice to make promises to people, even if we are not totally sure that we can keep that promise

_____

B. Make a fancy little card to give to someone. It could be a greeting card you make by hand or on the computer or an index card that you decorate. On the card, make a special promise to the person you are giving it to. Make sure it is something you will be able to do. Give the card to the person as a gift. Now, you have to keep your word and do what you promised!

MONTH 3

Take Care of Things

2 Chronicles 34:1-8

A. Do you have things to take care of? Almost everybody does. Maybe for you it is your belongings, like your clothing, schoolbooks or your toys. Maybe it is a pet. We would like you to think about how well you should take care of these things. In your Bible reading today, you read a little bit about one of the kings of Judah. His name was Josiah and he is a good example for you. He was only eight years old when he became king. You are probably near his age. Josiah did a lot of things right when he ruled God's people. First of all, he began to seek God while he was still young. We hope that you do that, too. Also, Josiah tried to take care of the things that belonged to his kingdom. He got rid of a lot of evil things and then he began to repair, or fix up, the Lord's house. That was a very good thing for him to do. You will probably never be a king or queen, but you should try to be responsible like King Josiah was. You should take very good care of the things that belong to you.

Write True or False:

Josiah was too young to do a good job as king.

B. On a piece of paper, make a list of some things you have to take care of. Next to each item on the list, draw a little picture of it. Show your list to your parents. Let them tell you how well they think you are taking care of these things.

Having Courage

Now we have come to the sixteenth day of the month. What shall we talk about? You can see that this is the day we will talk about having **courage**. Courage is the opposite of being afraid. When we say that someone has courage, it means that he or she is **brave**. It describes a person who is willing to do something difficult if it is necessary. You can be brave about many things, but we are going to think mostly about the kind of courage that makes you do what God wants you to do, even when it is hard or dangerous. We are going to think about three men in the Bible who had the right kind of courage, and we are going to talk about why they were so brave.

When You Pray

"Dear Jesus, I can only have courage if I trust you. Help me to trust in You and to be brave enough to do the right things. Amen."

Devotionals for Each Month

1. Daniel Had Courage
2. David Had Courage
3. Joshua Had Courage

MONTH 1

Daniel Had Courage

Daniel 1:8–16

A. On the fifth day of the month we talked about Daniel. We talked about how he kept on praying to God even when it put him in danger. Even before that happened, Daniel did something else that took a lot of courage. The king of the country where Daniel was living did not know God. Even though Daniel was young, he knew and loved the one true God and he wanted to obey Him. The king wanted Daniel and his friends to eat certain food that God had commanded them not to eat. What should Daniel have done? Well, he did a very brave thing. He asked the king's servant to allow him not to eat that food. God helped Daniel by giving the servant a friendly heart. He let Daniel and his friends eat just water and vegetables for ten days. God kept Daniel and his friends healthy. From then on they did not need to eat the food that would have been wrong for them to eat. Daniel was not afraid to do what was right, even before a king.

Are you ever afraid to do right? We hope that even if you are with your friends, your neighbors or your classmates, you will always be determined to do right, even if others do not. May the Lord give you the kind of courage that Daniel had.

Underline the right answer:

Why didn't Daniel want to eat the king's food?
a. He wanted to obey God.
b. The food did not taste good.

B. Sing the song "Dare to Be a Daniel" with your family tonight. Tell your family what you read about Daniel in your devotional today. Tell them of some ways you would like to be like Daniel.

MONTH 2

David Had Courage

1 Samuel 17:37,40–50

A. You knew this story already didn't you? Have you heard it a lot? When you read or hear about this story in the Bible, you probably always think about how brave David was. He was so young and so small to go fight such a big giant. The giant was a big **problem**. We all have problems—things that are hard for us. We can think of them as "giants" for us. David did not really kill his giant, God did. You can face *your* problems, even though you are young and small. You can face them for the same reason David could—it was God's battle, not David's. Your problems belong to God too, and that will hopefully give you courage.

Write True or False:

David was brave because he knew he was strong enough to defeat the giant. _____

B. On a piece of construction paper, draw a picture of David and Goliath. Make sure you show how big Goliath was next to David. On the back of the paper, draw another picture. Try to draw (or write about) something that

141

is a problem for you. Show your paper to your parents. Talk to them about why David could face the giant Goliath. Talk about how you can face *your* problem and why.

MONTH 3

Joshua Had Courage

Joshua 1:1–9

A. Joshua was a brave soldier. He fought many battles in the army of God's people. There are reasons why Joshua was so brave. It was because God had made promises to him. You just read what God said to Joshua after Moses died. Joshua was now the new leader of God's people. God made these promises so that Joshua would have courage to fight against God's enemies. Also, Joshua had seen God's power many times in the past and he had learned that God's people need His help to fight their battles. He also had learned that God's children can trust Him to help them. Your battles may not be the same as Joshua's, but we all have enemies who are real and who are strong, such as our sinful hearts and Satan, who tries to make us do wrong. We can trust God to give us faith and courage to fight these enemies.

Write in the word:

**Joshua was brave to fight his battles because
_____ was with him.**

B. Here is another hymn for your family to sing: sing "Who is on the Lord's Side?" together. It was written by a woman named Frances Havergal over one hundred years ago. Talk about the words of this hymn with your family members. Talk about the kind of battles God's children have today. Talk about any battles that you may have. Sometimes our enemy Satan attacks us to make us do wrong. He tries to get children to lie, cheat or be selfish or other things. Are you on the Lord's side? If you are, He will help you win the battles with your enemies. He will give you this very special kind of courage.

Caring

You would not say, "I don't care about anybody else," would you? You know that Jesus would be very sorry if you felt that way. When we talk about **caring** for other people, we mean the kind of care for others that makes us want to help them. We talked about kindness on another day and this is sort of like that. Now, we are thinking more about trying to *do* something for someone who has a need. We are thinking about showing **mercy** and **compassion** to others. This means that you feel bad about the sadness or hurt that someone else is having. You feel bad enough to help in any way you can. We sure do hope that you shine for the Lord this way.

When You Pray

Jesus said in Matthew 5:7: "Blessed are the merciful, For they shall obtain mercy." Pray for a heart of mercy and compassion. Learn this verse and live it whenever you can.

Devotionals for Each Month

1. Our Caring is for Jesus
2. Caring for All People
3. Caring for the Poor

MONTH 1

Our Caring is for Jesus

Matthew 25:31–46

A. Jesus is coming back again. Did you know that? He said He would, and He always does what He says. Your Bible reading today is telling you about that. It was a lot to read, but we wanted you to know it all. Jesus is talking about when He comes again. He talks about how He will put the people who belong to Him on one side and those who do not on the other side. He calls the people who belong to Him the "sheep." He tells how those who love Him will be with Him forever, but those who do not love Him will be punished. Do you see something interesting about Jesus' sheep? Do you see what kinds of things they do because of their love for Jesus? Sometimes they will feed hungry people or give clothes to people. Sometimes they will visit sick people or people in prison. That is what we want you to remember today. If you really belong to Jesus, it will show in what you do. And those who *do* belong to Him will do acts of kindness and mercy to people who are needy. In fact, the good deeds that we do for God's people are really being done for Jesus.

Circle the right answer:

Those who love Jesus are called (sheep / goats).

B. Another month we will talk about helping the poor. This month, we thought it would be nice if you would make plans to go see someone sick or shut-in. Maybe there is a shut-in neighbor nearby. You might go and see what you could do to help. Is there housework or yard work you could do? Talk to Dad or Mom about it. Maybe you could "visit" someone in a hospital or nursing home, or even in prison, by sending them a card. Make it by hand on nice paper or do one on the computer. Tell the person you send it to that you will pray for him or her and then make sure that you do.

MONTH 2

Caring for All People

Luke 10:25–37

A. All of us know someone who needs help. It could be someone who lives near us, goes to our school, or belongs to our church. Sometimes these people have a different skin color than we do or they speak a different language than we speak. Maybe they worship in a different way or even don't worship the true God at all. Should any of these things stop us from helping these people if we can? You know the answer: Of course not! Jesus often used stories called parables to teach about certain matters. The parable you just read teaches us that we should show kindness and be ready to help *anyone* who has a need, if we are able to. We should think of *all* people as our neighbors. The only one who helped the hurt man in the story was a man of another nation. This did not stop this man from helping a person that he saw needed help. We must remember to be like the Samaritan in the story. Is there anybody who needs *your* help?

Is this true?:
Our neighbors are only the people who live near us.

_____

B. There is a nice little poem which was written by Mr. John Wesley many years ago. It is called "Do Good," and we would like you to read it right now. It is located at Appendix B. Here is a writing assignment for you today: Copy this poem in your best handwriting on a nice piece of paper. Maybe you could draw a picture or two on the paper, as well. Maybe your picture could be of you doing something good. After you have finished, we are sure your parents will want to see it. Maybe all of you could pray together about this. Pray that your family will know what Jesus would want you to do to obey Him when He said "Go and do likewise," after He told this parable. Even though Jesus told this parable to a certain man, He wants all of us to listen as well.

MONTH 3

Caring for the Poor

Proverbs 14:31; 22:2

A. God is the Creator of each and every person. Some people are rich and some people are poor. God made all of them. Perhaps you are not very rich or not very poor. God made *you*, too. It is quite fine if you are neither poor nor rich. But there is something important that you need to know about those who are poor: God our Creator is very concerned about the way they should be treated. If we treat poor people wrongly, God will not be pleased with us. He will blame us as if we sinned against *Him*. This is similar to our devotional two months ago. If we truly love the Lord who made us and want to honor and please Him, we will care about those who are poor and we will do what we can to help them.

Write True or False:

Rich people are more important to God than poor people. _____

B. Find a magazine (from a Christian group) that shows pictures of very poor children. Many of these children are in other countries, but we have some in America, too. Pick one or a few of these children to pray for in a special way. Cut out their picture and put it up in your room. Think about sending a note to them, if possible. Think about putting away a little money in a special juice can with their name or names on it. Maybe you can think of little ways that you can earn nickels and dimes to put in that can. Later you could send the money to the group that helps that child or children.

Giving Cheerfully

"God loves a cheerful giver." We are sure that you have heard these words before. They are found at the end of 2 Corinthians 9:7, in the Word of God. These are words that we very much need to remember. Sometimes we don't like to give—we want to keep everything for ourselves. But that is not the way the Lord Jesus would want us to think. He wants us to give to others and to His work, and He wants us to be cheerful about it. He wants us to be willing to give and even to be thankful that we can give. Yesterday we talked about helping people in need. We are giving when we do that. Today we will think more about giving, especially giving to the Lord's work.

When You Pray

Memorize all of 2 Corinthians 9:7. Then pray for the Lord's help. He will help you to be happy to give when you can.

Devotionals for Each Month

MONTH 1

The Second Commandment

Exodus 20:4–6

A. Do you know what an **idol** is? An idol is not only a statue or image that people bow down to, it is *anything* that we love too much. Nothing should become so important to us that we love it more than God and His people. If that happens, it becomes an idol and we break the second commandment. The second commandment teaches us the proper, or right way, to worship God. Did you know that the Bible teaches that giving God at least one-tenth of our money is an important part of our worship? Sometimes money and the things we can buy with it become idols to people. Sometimes when people feel that way, they are not happy to give to God. We must be careful not to let that happen. We should not forget to give the Lord at least a tenth of all that we receive. If you earn or receive some money, make sure that you do not hold back from the Lord what should be given to Him. Whatever money can buy for you, it is <u>never</u> more important than God.

B. Have you learned about fractions in arithmetic yet? A fraction is a part of something, like one-half or one-fourth. If you haven't learned it yet, you will soon. What is one-tenth of something? Go find ten pennies and line them up. Take one of the pennies away. That penny is one-tenth, or one out of the ten parts. That is all God asks us to give to Him. That is not much, is it? We could really even give Him more if we wanted to. We hope that you give to God at least one-tenth of all that you receive. Here is another arithmetic problem: If you receive twenty pennies, how many should you give to the Lord?

MONTH 2

Giving for the Tabernacle

Exodus 35:21–29; 39:42–43

A. When God's people were wandering in the wilderness with Moses as their leader, God gave them an important job to do. He put them to work and had them build a place where they could worship Him. God told them all about how they were to make this tabernacle, which would be a tent that the people could put up and take down as they traveled. The people made this tent just as the Lord told them. The best part about it is that they gave with willing and happy hearts. They gave their things, their time, and their talents. Do you ever give *your* things, or time, or talents to Jesus? Do you ever have a chance to give to the work of His Church? Ask the Lord to help you to find ways that you can give of what *you* have. And when you have a chance to give, remember to do it with a willing and happy heart.

Circle the things that people gave to help make the tabernacle:

> wood animal skins jewelry talents time
> fine linen spices

B. With Legos or blocks, make a church building. While you are making it, think about the money that is needed to buy things to make such a building. Think about the time and talents people give to get the work done. After you finish making your church, think about what would need to be done to keep it nice for worship. Is there anything you can give or do to help keep things nice at the place where you worship?

MONTH 3

Everything Comes From God

1 Chronicles 29:9–16

A. We hope you enjoyed reading this Bible passage. You just read about King David as he was nearing the end of his life. God's people had been willing givers—they had cheerfully given their offerings so that David's son Solomon would be able to build a temple for the Lord God of Israel. What a good reason to give! David is giving praise to the Lord in the verses you just read. And as he is praising the Lord, he reminds the people of something very important. We *all* need to remember this: We need to remember that everything *belongs* to God and everything *comes* from Him. You need to be ready to give to Him cheerfully, because all that you have is really His anyway.

Put the letter of the correct sentence: _____

a. Some of what I have is mine and some is God's.
b. Everything I have is God's gift to me.

159

B. There is another hymn that you might want to sing with your family. This hymn was written by a man who was a minister. This man, Dr. Babcock, liked to go out and walk in the mornings. Do you like to go outside and play? When Dr. Babcock was outside, as he loved to be, he would think about nature and of his love for God, who created everything. So he wrote the song we call "This is My Father's World." When you and your family sing it, think about God as the Creator of everything, including you. Remember that everything in this whole wide world belongs to Him, including you. And remember that all that you have comes from Him. This is what we discussed with you at the very beginning of these devotionals. When you think about all that, we hope it will make you all the more happy to give to Him.

Doing Your Best

Now, you will agree, and we all will agree, that no one is perfect. To be **perfect** means that there is nothing wrong with you, you have no sin, and you do everything right. We all know that this is true only of our great God. Because we are just creatures and we are sinners, we will never be perfect in the way that God is. But God *does* expect us to try very hard to do our very best in everything. He wants us to do our best to be good, to do our best at our work, and to do our best to serve Him. Ecclesiastes 9:10 says, "Whatever your hand finds to do, do it with your might." That is what we mean when we say you should do your best. How brightly you will shine for Jesus if you do!

When You Pray

"Dear Jesus, whatever I try to do, help me to do my best. Help me to try very hard to do well and not to give up. And please help me to do whatever I do with all my might. Amen."

Devotionals for Each Month

1. Your Best Behavior
2. Your Best Work
3. Your Best Service

MONTH 1

Your Best Behavior

Luke 19:1–10

A. Does your mom ever say to you, "You'd better behave?" What does it mean to **behave**? When you behave, it means that you are trying to be good. You do what is right to do. At first, Zacchaeus was *not* good most of the time. He was a tax collector and sometimes he was not honest when he did his job. He even stole money from people. He did not behave. Then he met Jesus and Jesus changed his heart. After Jesus changed him, Zacchaeus tried his best to do right. He even wanted to give back money he had stolen from people. This was because Jesus had saved him and given him a new heart—a heart that wanted to be good. You must try *your* very best to be good. You must try to behave in ways that you know are right. Did you know that you cannot do this all by yourself? Did you know that if Jesus saves you, He will give *you* a new heart? Then, you would have *Him* help you to behave.

Put the right letter:
Why did Zacchaeus start trying to be good? _____
a. He was showing off.   b. Jesus changed his heart.

B. The only thing we want you to do today is to think about being good. What we mean is that we want you to think about how you behave. Do you try to do what is right? God is the only One who is always good and He helps children who belong to Him to try every day to please Him. Think about whether or not you belong to Jesus. He saved Zacchaeus and He can save you, too. Pray and ask Him to help you.

Do
Your
Best!

MONTH 2

Your Best Work

Genesis 6:22; Hebrews 11:7

A. Now let's talk about Noah. You probably already know a lot about Noah and the flood. Even when you were very little, you most likely heard the story. If you have not, read all about it in Genesis 6, 7, and 8. Today, however, we will not talk about the flood itself. We will think about the ark. People don't often think about what a hard job it was for Noah to build the ark. They don't think about the fact that it took him such a long time to build it. God had told him just what he was to do and just how the ark was to be made. Noah did exactly what God told him to do. He did not use short-cuts. A **shortcut** is a quick way to get a job done. He did not do that; he made sure he followed God's directions. If you are to do your best work, you should follow the instructions you are given and do it as carefully as you can. It may take you longer if you don't take shortcuts and you do your work neatly, but if you stick with it and do as you are instructed, you are doing your best work. And *that* pleases God.

Write True or False:

When Noah built the ark, he found a lot of shortcuts.

_____

B. When you find time, get a piece of construction paper. Write out Genesis 6:22 at the top. With colored pencils, draw a picture of Noah doing his best work in building the ark. On the back, draw a picture of you doing work that you have been told to do. When you do this work, how well do you follow the instructions from your parents and teachers? How carefully do you do it? Show the pictures to your parents.

Do
Your
Best!

MONTH 3

Your Best Service

Mark 14:3–9

A. The woman in the Bible story gave Jesus her best. She wanted to show her love to Him and that is what she did—by pouring out that expensive perfume on Him. Others who were there treated her as if she had done wrong. But not Jesus—He was pleased with what she did. He knew she did it out of her love for Him. She did the best thing she could think of. You can do that, too. You can serve Jesus by doing whatever you can to please Him and help with His work. Even the smallest little thing you do will make Jesus happy, if you do it with love in your heart and a desire to serve Him as best you can. See if you can think of something.

Do you agree?

We need to do our best to serve Jesus, even if it is something small. _____

B. We want to share our favorite rice pudding recipe with you. Maybe one day you could help make it. Maybe even today. You need four cups of milk, one-half teaspoon of salt, one-third cup of sugar and three table-spoons of regular rice. If you put in one-half teaspoon of nutmeg, it is *really* good. Put all of these items in a baking dish. It has to bake long. The oven should be 300 degrees and it bakes for about three hours or more. You want it to get nice and creamy. It smells very good while cooking. Now, why on earth are we talking about making a pudding? Well, perhaps this pudding will help you to think about a few things. Think about the salt and the sugar. When everything is mixed together, can you see the salt and sugar? Not really. But are they just as important as the milk and rice? What do you think? If you do some very small service for Jesus and mix it in with what others do, can all of those things together be meaningful? Maybe there are little errands you could run, or maybe you could help sort or pile books or pass out papers. See what you can do to help your parents, pastor or Sunday school teacher. Your little service can be added in to something very important. Just make sure that you do the very best that *you* can do in that little service.

Do Your Best!

Being Humble

Now we have some thoughts to share about being humble. God tells us in His Word that we must be humble. To be **humble** means that you do not think too highly of yourself. Yes, we know that you are yet a child. You probably feel that we do not need to tell *you* to be humble. And yes, we know that Jesus once said that people should humble themselves like little children. But that does not mean that children are never proud. What Jesus was saying was that grown-ups should have simple faith, like children often do. But when God teaches in the Bible that people should be humble rather than proud, He is talking about children, too. So today, let's think more about this.

When You Pray

Learn Matthew 11:28–29. These are Jesus' words. Was Jesus proud or humble? If He wants you for His crown, do you need to be proud or humble? Pray that He will make you what you need to be.

Devotionals for Each Month

1. God Brings Down the Proud
2. God Lifts Up the Humble
3. Do Not Praise Yourself

MONTH 1

God Brings Down the Proud

Daniel 4:28–35

A. First of all, do you know what it means to have pride or to be proud? A person is **proud** when he thinks that he is very important or that he is better than others. Sometimes proud people praise themselves and not God. That is what the King of Babylon did in your Bible reading. Did you have trouble reading his name? Someone may need to help you with that. But this is what we want you to learn about this king: When he walked around his palace (see verses 29 and 30), who was he giving praise to? That's right, he was praising himself wasn't he? And do you see what God did? He took away his great kingdom and made the king go live with animals. He even began to look and act like an animal! So you can see what God thinks of pride. Be careful that you are never proud like this king was. God might need to teach you a lesson, also. The good thing is that the king did learn his lesson and did end up giving praise to God.

Write True or False:

God can make proud people become humble.

_____

B. Read the Aesop's Fable called *The Tortoise and the Eagle* with your parents. Talk about how this story fits in with today's devotional. Read Proverbs 16:18 to your parents. Talk about it as a family.

MONTH 2

God Lifts Up the Humble

John 1:19–28

A. John the Baptist was Jesus' cousin. He and Jesus each had special work to do. God had even told their parents before they were born that they each had special work to do. Jesus, of course, was to be the Savior. And John the Baptist was chosen by God to tell the people the glad news that the Savior was coming. John was to tell the people to get ready to meet the Savior. And that was what he did. When he grew up, he did not live in a lovely palace. No, he lived in wild desert country, all by himself. He had no rich robes. He wore a coat of camel hair with a belt around his waist. He ate honey and locusts, not good food, like we eat. And he did his special work well. You can see some of the things he said in the verses you read. You can see how humble he was—he always pointed people to Jesus, not himself. What about you? Do you try to point people to yourself or to Jesus? If you are like John the Baptist, you do not think of yourself as more important than Jesus.

Put the correct letter:

How do we know that John the Baptist was humble?
a. He ate funny things.
b. He knew that Jesus was more important.

B. Luke 14:11 says: "He that humbles himself will be exalted." **Exalted** means to be lifted up. God has ways of "lifting up" humble people. John the Baptist was put in prison and killed by wicked persons. Was he lifted up when he went to Heaven? God has exalted other humble people by making them into leaders or kings or other rulers. But sometimes God simply finds ways to encourage them. During devotions with your family today, talk about ways that God exalts humble people. Pray that you will be like John the Baptist and Moses and others in the Bible who were humble. Also, there may be some famous missionaries or other workers for the Lord who would be good examples of godly, humble people who were exalted by the Lord.

MONTH 3

Do Not Praise Yourself

Proverbs 27:2

A. Remember the King of Babylon, who we talked about two months ago? Remember how he praised himself? You should never want to be like that. You should never want to be the type of person who brags about yourself and the good things you have or the good things you do. It is best to let others say whatever nice things there are to be said about you. Then it is all right. But even then, if others *do* say nice things about you, be careful not to let that make you think of yourself in a proud way. And remember, it is not all right to try to impress others by telling them how smart you are, how nice your hair is, or how well you play a game or sport or music. God does not want you to boast about yourself. So you need to be sure to obey this verse of Scripture.

Circle the answer:

**When we talk about the good things we do we are:
(being humble / bragging)**

B. Get out some puppets again. Maybe you could use the same ones that you used on the tenth day of last month or maybe you would like to use different ones this time. Anyway, pretend one of the puppets is very smart. Let's name the puppet Sparkey. Sparkey gets very good grades and has even won some spelling and math bees. Let's say Sparkey is also very good at sports and is very talented on the piano. Now, make Sparkey talk to another puppet. What kind of things would Sparkey say to the other puppet if he was bragging? What do you think the other puppet thinks of Sparkey? What does God think of Sparkey? Do *you* ever sound like Sparkey?

Keeping From Evil

"Evil" is a word that we do not like. It makes us feel bad inside when we hear that word. "Evil" is what Satan is, but it is also what Satan tries to make people be. He also tries to get people to *think* evil and *do* evil. Something that is **evil** is the opposite of what God is. God is all goodness, you know. Other words that mean the same thing as the word evil are words like "wicked" and "unrighteous." When people are **wicked** and **unrighteous** it means that they are very bad and they do wrong things. We hope that none of the children who read this book want to be wicked. Remember that it is only the Lord Jesus who can really keep you from evil.

When You Pray

Pray this prayer: "Dear Lord, please do not lead me into temptation, but deliver me from the evil one. In Jesus Name, Amen."

Devotionals for Each Month

1. Turn From Evil
2. Run From Evil
3. Say "No" to Evil

MONTH 1

Turn From Evil

Proverbs 4:14–19

A. A **path** is a trail or a track to walk on. You walk on a path to go from one place to another. In your Bible reading today, God is telling you that you must be very careful not to walk on any "path" that will lead you or take you to evil things. God is not talking about a real path when He says this. If you are at a place or with people and you see that being there will tempt you to do wrong, then that is the "way of evil." It is the "path of the wicked." God says it is like darkness. According to verse 15, we should not travel on that path; we should *turn* from it and go another way. If you do what pleases God and live for Him, then you are on the path that is a shining light, like the sun. That means you are being a bright gem! Make sure that you do not make friends who try to lead you to do wrong and that you don't look at bad things on TV or listen to the wrong kind of music or read anything that you should not read. These are all the "path of the wicked" and you must turn and go another way.

Circle the answer:

The way of the wicked is (shining / darkness).

B. You probably have a path at your house. It could be a walkway from the front to the back; it all depends on where you live. Maybe there is a sidewalk along the front. A sidewalk is a type of path. It is there so that people can safely walk beside a road. When a parent says it is okay, go outside and find a path or sidewalk to walk on. Take five or six giant steps on the path. Now play "imagine." Pretend you see three children ahead of you on the path. Pretend they are doing or saying wrong things. What should you do? You should turn and find another way to go, shouldn't you? You should not travel on this path because it could take you to evil. Find another path and hop or skip back to one of your parents and talk about what you have learned.

MONTH 2

Run From Evil

Genesis 39:7–12

A. This is another story that many children know well. Do you know it? If you do, you know that Joseph's brothers were jealous of him and sold him as a slave. That is how he got to Egypt as a slave in the house of a man named Potiphar. This man, Potiphar, had a wife who tried to get Joseph to break the seventh commandment. Now, we are not going to take the time to discuss the commandment itself. Maybe your parents will talk more about it with you. What we are wanting you to pay attention to is what Joseph did about it. We want you to be like Joseph. When this woman tried to get Joseph to sin, do you see what he did? Yes, he *ran* from her! That is what you must do if someone tries to get you to do evil: run away from it. When we **run** from something it does not *always* mean we should run with our feet like we do when we are in a race. Often it just means that we should get away as fast as we can. If anyone ever tries to get you to lie or cheat or steal or any other wicked thing, get away from them as fast as you can. Then ask Jesus to help you to *stay* away.

Fill in the word:

When Potiphar's wife tempted Joseph, he _____ from evil.

B. Later on, with the help of a grown-up, do this: Put about two quarts of <u>fresh</u> water in a bowl (you must start with fresh clear water each time). Then sprinkle black pepper onto the water in the bowl, so that there is some pepper sprinkled over the top of the water. Dip the end of a toothpick into some liquid detergent and then dip that same end of the toothpick into the center of the water sprinkled with the pepper. Watch the pepper "run" to the sides of the bowl! Let that be a reminder to you of how quickly you should get away from evil.

MONTH 3

Say "No" to Evil

Daniel 3:13–18

A. Remember Daniel? Remember how brave he was when he did not eat the food that the king wanted him to eat? Well, Daniel had three friends who were also brave. They had funny names—Shadrach, Meshach and Abednego. Can you say these names? These young men said "No" to the king. He wanted them to bow down and worship an idol he had made, and they would not do it. Good for them. They would only worship the true God. Because of this, the king did something awful. He threw them into a furnace of fire! Have you heard this Bible story before? If not, maybe your parents will tell you more. It is wonderful to read this story in the Bible and see how the Lord took care of these three young men so that the fire did not even hurt them. Because these three men said "No," even the king saw how great God is. If anyone ever tries to get you to do anything that would be sinful, you must always say "No." God will take care of you, too. There may be times when other children will try to get you to disobey your parents. You must always say "No." And make sure you seek God's help when you do.

Write True or False:

Daniel's three friends tried to please the king.

_____

B. Plan a little skit with other members of your family. Act out the Bible story you read today. Let there be one member of the family who does not know what the story is. Let that family member guess which story you are acting out. Explain to your family why Daniel's friends said "No" to the king. Also tell the others why these three men were right to disobey the king. Talk with your family about saying "No" to evil.

Being Loyal

If you really love someone or something you will be **loyal** to them. This is not just for grown-ups to think about. Children need to learn this early in life. Those you care about should be able to count on you. If you have friends, those friends should know that you will always be their friend, that you will be **faithful** to them. You will not change from day to day, wanting to be with them at certain times, and at other times not being nice to them. You will not say mean or unkind things about them to others and you will be there for them when they need your help. You will care about them at all times and want the best for them. That is what we mean when we talk about being loyal. You will be **true** to them. Be loyal to God, first. Also be loyal to your family, your friends, your church and your country. Don't grow up to be a person that others cannot count on to be true and faithful.

When You Pray

"Dear Lord, please help me to be loyal to You and to others. Help me to be faithful and true to those who love me and depend on me. Thank You that You are faithful to me. In Jesus' Name, Amen."

Devotionals for Each Month

1. Learn From King David
2. Learn From Jonathan and David
3. Learn From Ruth

MONTH 1

Learn From King David

1 Chronicles 28:9

A. King David was about to die and his son, Solomon, was to be king after him. David said many things to Solomon before he died. We wanted to let King David talk to you, too, so we had you read this verse in the Bible. Think very carefully about the words King David spoke to his son. These words are also for you while *you* are still young. David is reminding his son to be loyal to God. He is reminding his son that he should serve God always. He is also telling him to remember that God knows all about each of us. He wanted his son to know that he should seek God, and if he did, that he would find Him. He wanted his son to also know that if he would forsake, or turn from God, then God would turn from him. *You* need to know these things. *You* need to seek God while you are still a child and serve Him all of your life. Listen to the words of King David. Be loyal to your Father in Heaven.

Answer Yes or No:

Was King David being a good parent when he said all this? _____

B. Ask if your family can sing the hymn "Great is Thy Faithfulness" tonight, before you go to bed. Think about the words of this hymn. Don't you want to love and serve such a God who is so faithful to His people? Do you know if David's son, Solomon, did stay loyal to God? You can find out in 1 Kings 11. Ask one of your parents to read some of this to you. Is this a happy or sad chapter in the Bible? Ask your parents to talk to you about it. Do you want to be like Solomon?

MONTH 2

Learn From Jonathan and David

1 Samuel 18:1–4

A. Proverbs 17:17 says that "A friend loves at all times." In the Bible, Jonathan and David were like that. They loved each other and wanted to help each other. If one was in trouble, the other wanted to help. They were loyal friends. They even made promises to one another. They each promised that they would always help the other, and do all they could for each other. Even if one of them would die, they promised to help the children of the one who died. And do you know what? They were loyal and true friends because each kept his promise. Jonathan did all he could to protect David from King Saul, Jonathan's own father. After Jonathan had died and David became king, David did all he could to help Jonathan's son. You read about that on the ninth of last month. We hope that you will learn to be the kind of loyal friend that David and Jonathan were to each other.

Answer Yes or No:

Did Jonathan and David love each other at all times?

_____

B. One of Aesop's Fables is called *The Wolf and the Crane.* If you have it, read it with your family and talk about what makes a good friend. Think about which of the animals was <u>not</u> the kind of friend that you want to be. Were either of them *really* loyal to the other? Which animal made a promise? Did he keep his promise? Which animal tried to help the other? Did this animal have a good reason for helping? Do you try to help your friends? Do you try to keep your promises to them?

MONTH 3

Learn From Ruth

Ruth 1:15-18

A. There was a lady in the Bible named Naomi. She had two **daughters-in-law**. A daughter-in-law is the wife of someone's son. Naomi's husband had died and then her two sons died. You can read all about this in the Book of Ruth, in the Bible. The verses you just read were a part of that story. Naomi was from Israel, and she had been living in a country called Moab. Naomi decided to go home to Israel after her sons died, but her two daughters-in-law were from Moab. One of them wanted to go with Naomi at first, but then decided to stay in Moab. The other one, Ruth, did not leave Naomi. Ruth was so loyal and so devoted to Naomi that she said the things that you just read in verses 16 and 17. Ruth did go back with Naomi, and not only that, she stayed faithful to Naomi and to the one true God, the God of Israel. We hope you and your family can read the whole story one day and see how God blessed Ruth for her loyalty to Him and to Naomi. Let Ruth teach you to be loyal to your family, especially your parents. There are many ways for you to do this. You can be obedient and honest with those over you; you can be loving and caring to your brothers and sisters; and you can be helpful and responsible. All these are things we have already talked about. They are just *some* of the ways that you can show loyalty at home.

B. Draw another picture of all the people in your household. This time use colored pencils and construction paper. Make a nice pretty picture. Then, on the back, draw a picture of the place where your family worships for church. Here are some things to think and talk about after you make your drawings: In what ways are you loyal to your family? Are there ways that you could do better? After you show the drawings to others in your family, talk about how your family tries to be loyal to your church. Are there ways you could be more faithful? In what ways can you help your family and church to be loyal to your country?

Being Thankful

Thankful is what we should be when someone does something for us. It is what we should feel when something happens that makes us happy. It is when we appreciate what someone does for us or gives to us. Another word for thankful is the word "grateful." We always have a lot to be thankful for. As a child, you may sometimes forget this. We want to help you to remember how important thankfulness is. On another day, we talked about praying. Whenever you pray, always remember to give praise and thanks to God. Even before you ask Him for anything, you should thank Him and praise Him.

When You Pray

Pray this prayer: "Dear Lord, thank You for all my blessings; thank You for providing for my needs; and thank You most of all for Jesus. In His Name, Amen."

Devotionals for Each Month

1. Be Thankful for Your Blessings
2. Be Thankful God Provides
3. Say "Thank You"

MONTH 1

Be Thankful for Your Blessings

Psalm 107:8

A. Most of us have things which can be called blessings. A **blessing** is something that is good to have. It is something that makes you happy or contented. It is something that God favors you with. It is also called a **benefit**. If you have a house to live in, that is a blessing. It doesn't matter that much if it is a little house or a big house, it is still a blessing. If you have parents, that is a blessing. Brothers and sisters are blessings. So are grandparents. Do you go to a nice church? If you do, that is a blessing, too. If you have a nice school to go to or if you are able to have school at home, these are blessings as well. If you have a mind that can learn to read, write and learn numbers, that is also a blessing. You probably have lots and lots of other things that are blessings. It is very important that you thank God for all that He has done for you and given to you. If you are a Christian, the very best blessing that you have is the Lord Jesus. We must always remember to thank God for Him.

Finish the sentence:

God gives most people many _____.

B. Why not sing a song all by yourself today? Do you know the song "Count Your Blessings?" Maybe you could walk around your house singing it for a little while today. Maybe others will join in with you. Even if you don't know the whole song, sing the part that says "Count your blessings, name them one by one. Count your blessings, see what God has done. Count your blessings, name them one by one. Count your many blessings... See what God has done!" Name some of the blessings you have and then thank God for each one.

MONTH 2

Be Thankful God Provides

Numbers 21:4–6

A. Remember on the thirteenth of last month when we talked about trusting God? It was then that we talked about how our Heavenly Father provides food for us to eat and clothes for us to wear. When you think about this, we hope this makes you very thankful. After God's people left Egypt where they had been slaves, they were headed to the land God had promised them. During the time they were traveling, God took care of them and sent them special food called "manna." It was sometimes called "bread from Heaven." This food fell from Heaven, and God sent it every day except the Sabbath. On the day before the Sabbath, God also sent enough for the Sabbath Day. What a wonderful way the Lord provided for His people! When you read your Bible reading today, did God's people sound thankful? No, we are sorry to say, they did not. It's sad to read what they said isn't it? God was angry with them and punished them. Are you thankful for God's care of you? Do you tell Him you are thankful? Every time you sit down to eat a meal you should thank Him, even if you are eating out. It would even be nice if we would sometimes say a thank you to Him for our clothes when we get dressed in the morning!

Write the answer:

Who gave food to God's people as they traveled?

_____

B. Make a meal out of playdough later today. Invite a few people to share your food. Make a table up to look nice for those who are coming. Before everyone pretends to eat, say grace and thank God for the food. Is this what you do when you eat your real meals? Here is a nice verse to hide in your heart: Psalm 145:15. Maybe you can recite it at some of your meals.

MONTH 3

Say "Thank You"

Luke 17:11–19

A. We talked about the disease of leprosy at another time. It was such a bad skin disease that the people who had it were called unclean and they had to keep away from other people. People with leprosy are called **lepers**. In the Bible story, there were ten men who were lepers. Jesus healed them all. How many came back to thank Jesus? That's right, just one came back to say "thank you" and Jesus was very pleased with that one leper. He was *not* pleased with the other nine. Jesus is pleased with *you* when you take the time to say "thank you" when someone does something for you. Be sure to do this. Thank your dad and mom for all they do for you. If others have you over, thank them. If someone gives you something, thank that person. Thank your teacher or mom or Sunday school teacher for teaching you. Whenever you thank another person, it is even better when you say <u>what</u> you are thanking them for. Jesus loves it when children use the special words of "thank you."

True or False:

Jesus was pleased with nine of the lepers He healed.

_____

B. A very good way to thank someone is to give that person a thank you card. Make a card for one of the people we talked about today. Write that person a little note saying "thank you" and tell them just what you are thanking them for.

Being Unselfish

L et's think about something that often keeps children from shining bright for Jesus: selfishness. Because of the sin in our hearts, this is a very big problem. It is a problem for children even from the time they are little babies. We all start out caring about ourselves more than anyone else. If you are like most people, you have this problem, too. It is hard not to think of yourself first and to want the best for yourself. It's hard not to want the best of something or the most of something good. Often it's hard not to keep everything, instead of sharing it with someone else. Jesus was not selfish when He was here on earth. He gave His very best for others. We want to try to be like Him. Even though it is hard, He can help us to be unselfish.

When You Pray

Pray for help: "Dear Jesus, only You can help me with the selfishness in my heart. Help me to learn to love others as much as I love myself. This is what you have said I must do. Help me to obey You in this. Amen."

Devotionals for Each Month

1. Share With Others
2. Think of Others
3. Put Others First

MONTH 1

Share With Others

Mark 12:41–44

A. When we give to poor, sick or helpless people, we call that **charity**. When we give to any kind of charity, we are sharing what we have with others. Jesus saw some people giving at the temple. Some people who were rich gave a lot, but they had so much that they only gave a small part of what they had. Jesus was very pleased with what He saw a poor widow give. It was only a little, but she only *had* a little and she gave *that* to help others. Wasn't that a very unselfish thing to do? You will make Jesus pleased with *you* if you share with others. You can give to charity, but there are other ways you can share, as well. Letting someone play with your toys is sharing. You share when you give someone something that belongs to you. You also share when you help someone learn something that you know how to do. A child who likes to share is a blessing to others. We hope this is true of you.

Underline the answer:

Who really gave the most of what they had?
(the widow / the rich people)

B. Let's hear you count to 100. Pretend somebody gave you that many lollipops. Pretend that you share five of them with a friend. That's very nice of you. Now pretend someone gave you two lollipops and you share one of those with your friend. It was nice of you to share both times, but even more so when you shared just the one lollipop. Maybe there is something even better than lollipops that you have to share with others, even if you only have a little. By sharing a part of that little you have, you could be a real blessing to someone else.

MONTH 2

Think of Others

Philippians 2:3–4

A. Who is the most important person in all the world? If you are a selfish child, you think *you* are. But of course you are not, you know. Others are just as important as you are. This is something each and every one of us needs to understand. In fact, God tells us that we should even think of others as being *more* important. The Bible teaches that you must not just think about what *you* need and what *you* want. You must also think about what others need and want. How can you love others as Jesus commanded if you only care about yourself? Be a bright and shining jewel for Jesus by showing others that they are just as important as you are. There are many ways that you can do this. Did you ever get to go somewhere that a friend would have liked to have gone? If you try <u>not</u> to go on and on about the good time that you had when you are around that friend, are you being thoughtful? Did you ever <u>not</u> do something so that a brother or sister could do it instead? Now, *that* is being unselfish. Ask for wisdom from the Lord for other ways to think of others.

Write True or False:

The Bible teaches us that we should think only of ourselves _____

B. There is an Aesop's Fable which is called *The Dog in the Manger*. Some people think this little fable is funny because they say so many people are like this dog. That is true, you know, but people who are so selfish that they don't think about the needs of others are usually not funny at all. We hope you are able to read this fable and talk about it with your family. Whatever you do, make sure that you do not grow up to be that kind of person. Let the dog be a bad example for you. If you are ever able to watch birds or squirrels at a feeder you will see that they are often like the dog in the manger. See how bad that looks? We hope that you are never like that and never will be.

MONTH 3

Put Others First

Esther 4:16-17; 5:1–2

A. Earlier last month we thought about Queen Esther. Remember when we talked about her self-control? What she did was scary for her. But she did it anyway because it was the right thing to do. We could even have talked about her when we talked about having courage. But there is another thing we could say about Queen Esther. When she went in to see the king, who was she putting first—herself or others? She was thinking first of others wasn't she? She knew her people were in danger. She also knew that it was possible she could help them. She *also* knew that she could be killed for going in to see the king without being called. This is another way you can be like Queen Esther. You can be like her by putting others first. You don't have to do anything as dangerous as what Esther did. You could try letting a friend go ahead of you in a game, or you could let someone else have the first choice of a cookie. Perhaps you could think of a way to put your mom first. Remember, she usually puts *you* first. With the Lord's help, you can think of other ways to be unselfish by putting others first.

Write the answer:

Who was Esther putting first? _____

B. You probably have learned about **ordinal numbers**— first, second, third and so on. Get five or six stuffed animals or beanies. Pick one of them and pretend it is you. The others are your friends. Line them up and pretend they are going to do something that is a lot of fun or that they are going to get something yummy. Who will you have go first? Or who should get the first choice? Why? Someone would need to be second, third, fourth and fifth. Someone would need to be last. Would you and your friends have an argument over it? Is that what usually happens? Show your little lineup to a parent and explain it to him or her.

Not Being Envious

Envy is a sin that we see quite a lot. We even see this sin among those who are Christians. Even children are often envious. It is a very sad sin and we wish we did not see it as much as we do. When we **envy** others we do not like it when they have something good or nice or if they do something well. We do not like it if something good happens to them. Sometimes people are envious when someone else looks a certain way. When we envy others, we are **jealous** of them. On this day of the month we will discuss how envy and jealousy can hurt us and hurt others. We will talk about how God wants us to feel about the good things that others have and do.

When You Pray

Pray that God will take the sin of envy and jealousy out of your heart. Ask Him to help you to be happy about His good favor to others.

Devotionals for Each Month

1. Envy Hurts You and Others
2. Be Happy for Others
3. Envy is Not From God

MONTH 1

Envy Hurts You and Others

1 Samuel 18:5–9

A. Saul was king of Israel. David was one of his soldiers. From what you read today, what kind of soldier would you say that David was? Was he a good one or a bad one? How did he act? Was he a faithful or unfaithful servant for his king? How did all the people feel about him? Read the verses carefully and you will be able to tell. Yes, David was a faithful, wise, obedient and brave soldier. So why in the world was King Saul upset with him? You guessed right—it was because of envy. Saul did not like what the women sang in verse 7 and because of that, he ended up first envying, then being angry and, after a while, even hating David. As time went on, he even started trying to kill David. Saul's envy made him a sad and angry man. Envy could do that to you, too. *You* could end up being sad and unhappy and then being mean to those you envy. Many times children become jealous of their brothers or sisters or their friends. Please do not let this happen to you. If you feel jealousy creeping into your heart, pray and ask God to take it away.

Underline the correct answer:

Saul was angry with David because:
a. David was not a good soldier.
b. Saul was envious of David.

B. Ask your mom to help you find a piece of fruit or vegetable that is going bad. Or maybe you could find a plant that has leaves that are coming off and starting to rot. Ask your mom to tell you what is going to happen to that rotting fruit or the rotting leaves. Then ask one of your parents to read Proverbs 14:30 with you. Ask them to explain how envy is like the rotting that you looked at today.

MONTH 2

Be Happy for Others

Romans 12:10,15

A. Now this may seem strange to you, but did you know that it is often hard to be happy when someone else is happy? Very often it is easier to be sad when someone else is sad. Do you know why this is sometimes true? It is because of envy. If something good happens to your friend or your friend's family and they are very happy, can you be happy too? Can you rejoice with that friend? If you do not envy that person, you will be glad for him or her. All of this has to do with loving others. Remember before when we talked about loving others? When you read Romans 12:10 today, you could see that the Lord wants you to desire the best for others and to even prefer them. This means you should not mind if they have something better than you or something you don't have. It makes you happy to see them happy. This is a Christian grace (or fruit) that the Lord can give to you if you really seek it from Him.

Circle the answer:

When others are happy, we should be (happy / sad).

B. Today we would like you to design your own post-cards. We want you to make four or more of these postcards. Use four-by-six plain index cards. Using your colored pencils or markers, draw a nice picture on one side of each index card. It could even be a happy picture of yourself. On the other side of the index card, draw a line down the middle. On the right side of the line, you will put a person's name and address. On the left side of the line, you will put your message. These postcards are to send to friends. You should only use these cards to send a happy message when something good happens to them and you want to say how happy you are for them. Send one today if there is someone you can rejoice with. Don t forget—you need a postage stamp!

MONTH 3

Envy is Not From God

James 3:13–16

A. If anybody has envy in his or her heart, you can be sure that God did not put it there. If a heart of envy does not come from Heaven, you can guess that people who envy are not being like Jesus. They are being like Satan. And it is *Satan*, not Jesus, who is happy when we are envious of others. After all, Satan does not like it that God rules over everything. He does not like it when people praise and worship God. That is the spirit of envy, and Satan would like us to be like that, too. He likes it when we do not like others to do well or have honor or praise. Did any of your friends get something new lately? Maybe they got a new brother or sister? Or a house? Or did any of them get praised for doing well at something, such as their grades or maybe playing music or sports? You did not make Satan happy, did you? If you did <u>not</u> have a heart full of jealousy about it, you made *Jesus* happy and we hope that is what you want to do!

215

Answer the question:

If something good happens to someone else and you are envious of them, who is happy, God or Satan?

———————

B. Later in the day, read the Aesop's Fable *The Raven and the Swan.* Sometimes it is called *The Crow and the Swan.* Draw a picture of the two birds as they would have looked at the beginning. What was in the heart of the raven that made him do what he did? If the raven had been a person, who might have put those feelings in his heart? What happened to the raven? Why did this happen? Ask your parents to explain to you how this story can help you to understand today's devotional and the one two months ago.

Forgiving Others

Do you know what it means to forgive someone? Suppose a person does something wrong that hurts you. Maybe a friend says something mean to you or calls you a bad name. People often do unfair things that cause us to be sad or upset. To **forgive** someone who has hurt us means that we stop being angry or bitter towards the one who has done the wrong against us. We try to forget about it. We try to stop being upset with him for what he has done. Jesus is the best One to teach us about forgiveness. He taught us about forgiveness when He preached and showed us how to forgive by His example.

When You Pray

Memorize Ephesians 4:32. If you are upset or angry with anyone who has done wrong to you, pray that the Lord will give you a heart of forgiveness toward that person.

Devotionals for Each Month

1. Jesus Teaches Forgiveness in the Lord's Prayer
2. Jesus Teaches Forgiveness in a Parable
3. Stephen Learned Forgiveness From Jesus

MONTH 1

Jesus Teaches Forgiveness in the Lord's Prayer

Matthew 6:9–15

A. In the Lord's Prayer, Jesus taught us to forgive our "debtors." He is talking about those who have sinned against us. Your Bible may say they have "trespassed" against us. They have done something against us. Think about your friends. Suppose one of them was mean to you one day. Let's call him Alex. Suppose he said to you "You're ugly and I don't like you." That was a very mean and unkind thing that Alex said. He hurt you; he sinned against you. Would you be right to tell your mom that you will never forgive Alex and that you will never be his friend again? If you stayed angry with Alex and would not talk to him, you would be holding a grudge. That would be a sin, too. You would need to forgive Alex in your heart. Someday maybe you could talk to him and you could be friends again. No matter what, you should be praying for Alex. You should pray that God would change his heart towards you. *You* have sinned against God. Would God say He never wants to be your Friend? Ask Him to forgive you and He will. Ask Him to change *your* heart and He will. Then He will help you to be forgiving of others.

219

Write True or False:

According to the Lord's Prayer, our "debtors" are people who owe us money. _____

B. We are pretending that the dog on this page has done something wrong. He could have chewed someone's shoe or something like that. Maybe he will need to be corrected and taught to do better, but if he were *your* dog, you would probably forgive him. Wouldn't you do the same for a person? You wouldn't hold a grudge against him, would you? Being forgiving is very important. Talk to your parents about verses 14 and 15 in today's Bible reading. Draw a picture of the dog after he is forgiven by his owner.

MONTH 2

Jesus Teaches Forgiveness in a Parable

Matthew 18:21–35

A. You remember what a parable is, don't you? It is a story that has a lesson. Remember? The parable you read today was about a servant who did not forgive another servant who owed him money. The one who owed money could not pay it back to the first servant. The first servant did not forgive the one who owed the money. That means he did not say to him, "I can see that you are unable to pay, so I will not make you pay." Instead, he put the servant who owed him the money into prison. This was really wrong because the man who was master over the servants had already told the first servant that he did not have to pay *him* (the master) what was owed. The parable teaches that the master was angry with the first servant for the way that he had treated his fellow servant. How does our Heavenly Father feel about us if we do not forgive others when they sin against us? Learn from this parable. God has forgiven you many times. You need to do the same for those who have hurt you. Some of these people could be friends, but they could even be members of your own household. No matter who they may be, it is extremely important that you be as forgiving toward them as God has been to you.

Write down how often we should forgive another person (see verses 21 and 22): _____

B. Here is a project for you today: Make stick puppets of the three men from the parable: Draw the master and the two servants on construction paper. Next, color them. Then cut them out and glue the figures on Popsicle sticks or straws. Give the men pretend names if you wish. After you have made up the puppets, use them to act out what happened in today's story. Present your little play to some of your family. Talk about why the first servant was wrong. We would also like to suggest that you make stick puppets of some children. Make up a story using the children puppets to show what you learned today.

MONTH 3

Stephen Learned Forgiveness From Jesus

Acts 7:54–60

A. It is possible that you have learned about Stephen in your Sunday school class. Stephen was a very godly man who was one of the first deacons to serve in God's Church. In your Scripture reading, you could see that he was killed by wicked people because of his love for Jesus. These wicked people hated Jesus and they were angry at Stephen for telling others about Jesus. So one day they threw big stones at Stephen until he died. These people who killed him were his enemies, and what they did was evil. But Stephen prayed for them even as he was dying. Do you see what verse 60 says? Stephen asked God not to hold their sin against them. He prayed for those who were killing him. Do you know who else did that? If you answered that it was the Lord Jesus, you are right. Jesus also prayed for those who were killing Him. Stephen probably learned from Jesus. You should learn the same lesson. The next time someone does some wrong against you, pray for that person. Try to remember that no matter how much others may have hurt you, Jesus would want you to pray for them and forgive them.

Circle the answer:

When dying, both Jesus and Stephen (cursed / prayed for) their enemies.

B. Before you go to bed tonight, ask one of your parents to read Matthew 5:44 to you. Talk about this verse with your parent and talk also about the story today. Talk about what lessons you have learned about forgiveness. Is there any particular person that you are having a hard time forgiving? Now is a good time to pray for him or her.

Not Complaining

There is a very bad habit that many children have: they complain. They complain about having to do school-work; they complain about having to wait; they complain about their brothers and sisters; they complain if they don't get something that they want; and on and on and on. Pouting and whining are favorite ways children have of complaining. You are definitely not a sparkling jewel when you complain. If you spend more time learning to be thankful and patient and content, you will have little time left to complain.

When You Pray

Ask God for His grace to keep you from a complaining spirit. Ask Him to help you to be more thankful, patient and content. Ask Him to help you not to get into the habit of whining or pouting. Keep praying about this over and over if you have to.

Devotionals for Each Month

1. Obey in Your Heart
2. Do Not Pout
3. That's Not Fair!

MONTH 1

Obey in Your Heart

Philippians 2:14–16

A. Betty grumbles every time her mother asks her to watch her toddler brother. Kevin complains about his homework when he does it. When Paul does his piano practice, he grumbles while he is doing it. Lynette always does her chores, but she grumbles and complains about having too many of them. Most of the time, Gail complains that her Bible memory work is too hard, even though she usually can say the verses when the time comes. These children are all obeying their parents and teachers by their actions, but they are not happy to be obeying. Do you ever grumble about any of these things? Do you do what you are told to do, but all the while complain about it? If so, pray that the Lord Jesus will help you to obey in your heart without complaining. After reading these Bible verses, you can see that complaining keeps us from shining as lights in the world, even when we are *doing* the right things.

Do you agree?
It does not matter if we grumble about doing something , as long as we get it done. _____

227

B. Later on, draw a picture on your chalkboard or dry-erase board. Draw yourself doing something you often complain about doing. Then, write on the board the words you *should* say or think the next time you have to do whatever you drew. Show your drawing to your dad or mom.

MONTH 2

Do Not Pout

1 Kings 21:1–7

A. A little girl named Mary wanted to go to the park one day, but her mother was too busy to take her. All through lunch Mary had a sour look on her face and she was quite unpleasant to be around for the rest of the day. In fact, even though she was often a lovely girl to look at, with her lips pushed out and the little frown on her face, she was not pretty at all. Mary was pouting. Pouting is another way to complain. You can see that Mary was acting like King Ahab, who was sulking and pouting because his neighbor Naboth would not give him his vineyard. You only read a part of the story. Actually, many bad things happened after Ahab started pouting about Naboth's vineyard. Many sins were committed by many people until finally Naboth was killed. It all started with Ahab's coveting and then his pouting. And God judged Ahab after all was said and done. Pouting and sulking are very ungodly ways to behave. *None* of us can always have everything we want. Don't be like Ahab. Don't pout. God will not like to see your face that way.

True or False:

King Ahab's pouting turned out to be very harmful.

_____

B. Later today, stand in front of a mirror. Make a happy smiling face at yourself. Then make a sad face. Then make an angry face. Finally, look at yourself with a pouting, sulking face. Which face shines the brightest for Jesus? Which face is a complaining face? Do you like looking at it? The next time you cannot have what you want, will you have a complaining face?

MONTH 3

That's Not Fair!

Matthew 20:1–16

A. One thing children often say is "No fair!" Maybe *you* have said that. That is actually what the workers in the parable really meant. Some were hired early to do the work and some were hired very late and didn't have to work as long. The owner paid them all the same amount. What do you think about that? Are you saying that wasn't fair? But do you see what the owner said in verse 13? The first workers got what they were supposed to get. So they should not have complained that others got the same. Sometimes things will not seem to be fair. But if you do your part and try your best to do what is expected of you, then God will be pleased. If you know that you are pleasing God, *that* is the reward you want. So always trust the Lord to give you what is best for *you*, even if someone else gets more than you might think they should. Remember, now, if sister or brother gets to stay up later or gets to go somewhere special or gets a bigger present, don't say, "That's not fair!"

Answer Yes or No:

In the parable, did the owner give the first workers what he had promised them? _____

B. This evening, see if you can play a board game with some of your family. A good one would be one that has a spinner that spins to different numbers. Or it could be a game that has dice you roll. After the game is over, somebody will more than likely be the winner. Who decided who would win? Who decides everything? Is there really such a thing as luck or chance? Should the people who did not win say that it was not fair? Why or why not? Can you trust that God will always do what is right in other more important matters? Will it always seem fair to you? Discuss all of these questions with your family after you play the game.

Being Content

Now, if we can learn to stop complaining, we are on our way to being content. That is sometimes very difficult. Very often we want *other* than what God has given us or we do not like the *way* God has made us or we want *more* than God has given us. Sometimes things are not going the way we want them to or there is something we have to wait for. At this time in your life, while you are still so young, pray that the Lord will help you to see that He knows best. He can help you to be a happy and contented child, whether you have a little or a lot, no matter what you look like and no matter if there is something that is not quite as you would like it to be. If you truly love Him, you are a precious jewel shining for Jesus and what could be better than that?

When You Pray

"Lord Jesus, thank you for loving me enough to always do what is best for me. Help me to trust you and to be content. Amen."

Devotionals for Each Month

1. The Tenth Commandment
2. God the Potter
3. About Greed

MONTH 1

The Tenth Commandment

Exodus 20:17

A. Let's think about the tenth commandment and what it really means. First, we need to understand what it means to **covet**. In the tenth commandment, God says that we are not to covet what belongs to our neighbor. All the different people that we know are our "neighbors." We should not be always wishing we had what others have. Also, we are not to have strong desires in our heart for more than what God has given to us. We have already talked about envy. Coveting and envy are very much alike. We should be satisfied with our gifts from God, no matter how small they are. This means that we should be **content** with our lot. Our "lot" is the portion, or share, that God gives to us. This commandment teaches that we should be satisfied, or content, with that. So, if God has given you a big, small or medium sized house, He wants you to be thankful for it. Whatever the size of your family, He does not want you to look at someone else's family and be discontented with yours. We need to try very hard to obey this command. Yes, we know this is hard at times. We all struggle not to covet. We need to ask Jesus to forgive us if we do. We need to ask *Him* for contentment.

Underline the best word:

When we covet, we are not being (content / envious).

B. On the twenty-third of the month, we asked you to name some of the blessings that you have and to thank God for each one. Today, we would like you to *really* count your blessings and to name them one by one. It would be nice if you would take a piece of paper and make a list of your blessings from God. Draw a little picture beside each one. Talk about these blessings with your parents. Did the Lord give you the same blessings that He has given to others? Do you think He knows best what to give to each person? How can this help to give you more contentment?

MONTH 2

God the Potter

Isaiah 64:8

A. Have you ever seen a potter work? He takes clay and makes things out of it. He forms it just the way he wants it to be. The Bible calls God our Potter. It says that we are the clay. That means He makes us just the way *He* wants us to be. Some children have brown hair, some black, some blond or red. Some have thick hair and some have thin hair. Your skin color may be brown or white or some other color. You may be growing taller or shorter than others your age. There may be many other things about you that make you different from other people. God the Potter made you the way you are. You belong to Him as your Creator and He made you to look like *He* wants you to look. He wants you to be content with how He made you and not to wish you were like someone else. Never grumble about these things. If you do, you are grumbling against God.

True or False:

God the Father is called our Potter because He created us. _____

B. Take some time today to use your playdough. Make a few little pots and bowls different shapes and sizes. Set them out in a row and admire them. Can these pots and bowls complain to you about how you made them? Can they themselves change what you have done? Should you complain to God the Potter about how He made *you*? Why or why not? Can you change what He has done? Talk with your dad and mom about what this teaches you about being content.

MONTH 3

About Greed

Luke 12:15-21

A. At some time or another, your mother has probably said to you, "Don't be greedy." Maybe you already had a dish of ice cream and you had plenty the first time, but you want another helping. You don't *really* need it, but you just want more. Very often when that happens, it is greed. You can be greedy about anything—you want more clothes, more time to play, more toys or even more attention from others. **Greedy** means that even though you may have enough of something, you are not satisfied, or content, with what you have. You want more of it. You just read this story in the Bible about a man who was greedy. He was rich but he wanted to get richer. He was selfish, too, because he didn't want to share what he had with others. Instead of sharing, he decided that he would build bigger barns so that he could keep his riches all to himself. Greedy people are usually not happy because they are never content. The Lord Jesus will help you to be content with what He gives you if you ask Him to. Then, perhaps you can use what He's given to you to help others to be happy.

Underline the correct words:

The man in the Bible story was (greedy, selfish, hungry, happy).

B. There is another little interesting story about a dog. It is also one of Aesop's Fables and it is about a dog that had some meat. In some books it is called *The Dog and the Shadow* and in other books it is called *The Dog Carrying Meat*. We hope you are able to read this fable with a parent so that you might talk about it afterward. Talk about why the dog ended up with no meat at all. Talk about what the main problem was that caused this to happen. Did anything like this ever happen to you? What finally happened to the man in the Bible story? What have you learned from all this?

Having Good Manners

"Mind your manners!" says your mom, as you go over to your friend's house to spend the day. What are **manners**, anyway? For one thing, manners can be good or bad. We will talk about *good* manners today. We will think about showing **courtesy** to others. Having good manners, or being courteous, means you will be thoughtful of others, you will be polite. It also means you will be kind and considerate to them and respect their feelings. On the twenty-third, we talked about being thankful. Showing and expressing thankfulness are important types of good manners. In other words, good manners really have to do with caring about others, not just yourself. They have to do with showing love to others— so you know from *this* that Jesus wants you to have good manners.

When You Pray

Like all Christian graces, we need to pray for help in having good manners. Whether you are a boy or a girl, pray for wisdom and patience to know how to be more courteous.

Devotionals for Each Month

1. Courtesy in Speech
2. Being Considerate
3. Do Unto Others

MONTH 1

Courtesy in Speech

Colossians 4:6

A. *What* we say and *how* we say it is such an important part of good manners that we will talk about that, first. You probably already know how important the words "please" and "thank you" are. But there are other things you need to remember. Since you are yet a child, learning how to speak to grown-ups is a big part of having good manners. You must remember to always show respect when you talk to an adult. Now, think about what you do and say when someone older talks to *you*. Do you mumble "Uh-Huh" or "Unh-Unh"? Or do you sometimes answer with "yeah"? Please, please never do that. Even just answering with a single word is not really good enough. The best thing is to say something like "Yes, sir" or "No, ma'am" or "Hello, Mr. Jones." If you say "Yes, I do," that is better than just yes. Do you see how much more respectful that sounds? And as for other children, be courteous in how you speak with them, also. Never make fun of others and don't ever whisper to one person when there are others present. That is rude and unkind. Always think about how you will make others feel. (Remember what we said on the ninth and tenth of the month.) Be courteous to others in your speech.

243

Do you agree?:

Knowing how to talk to others is also good manners.

_____

B. A puppet show would be good for today's study. When you can, get out or make some puppets. Do a quick little show for your family later today or this evening. Have one puppet be a grown-up and two puppets be children. Let the grown-up (Mr. Jones) talk to the children. Give the children names. Let one child have good manners and the other bad manners. Show how each would talk to Mr. Jones. Which of the children are you usually like? Which one do you want to be like?

MONTH 2

Being Considerate

1 Peter 3:8

A. Dad and Mom are having an important conversation. In comes Bobby, who loudly asks, "Mom, may I have a Popsicle?" Another time, Mom is on the phone talking to a friend. Bobby picks this time to ask his mother a question about his truck. Sometimes, at church, Bobby rushes between or in front of people without saying anything to them. Is Bobby being considerate? No, of course not. He is being rude, isn't he? To be **considerate** means you care about others when you do something. You care about how your actions will affect someone else. If you remember what we said about unselfishness, you will see that this is a little like that. All of the different character traits that we have discussed work together, don't they? Bobby needs to learn good manners. He should not plunge in when others are talking. He should wait for a better time to ask for something. If he *must* ask it, he should at least say "excuse me," first. He should say the same thing if he walks in front of people. And he should never walk between people who are talking unless he *really* has to. But if he must, he should *definitely* ask them to please pardon or excuse him. Here, again, we can see how we need to think about others. Also, young people like yourself can have good manners by getting up and giving your seat to an older person. Also, maybe you could get something for them without being asked. *That* is being considerate, and don't you think it is pleasing to God?

True or False:

If you are considerate, you will care about others.

_____

B. Do a role play of Bobby today—you pretend that you are Bobby. Have a couple of other people act out the roles of others. Have Bobby do some of the things we talked about today. In the skit, show how Bobby would have made the other people feel. Show how Bobby could have been more considerate. It would be nice to have a little family talk about all of this.

MONTH 3

Do Unto Others

Matthew 7:12

A. Would you like it if someone talked to you with a lot of food in his mouth? Do *you* like looking at chewed up food? How would you feel about your friend sneezing or coughing on you without covering his mouth? Would *you* like getting sprayed by him? What about the friend who reaches across you and takes the last chocolate chip cookie when *you* wanted it? How would you feel about *that?* There is something called the "Golden Rule." It says, "Do unto others as you would have them do unto you." The Bible verse you just read is really saying the same thing. If you follow this rule, will you have good manners? It certainly would be a help, that's for sure. If you did follow this rule, you probably would be careful to eat with your mouth closed so your food doesn't show. You wouldn't sneeze or cough on people. And you would <u>not</u> snatch up the last of something good without caring if someone else wanted it. If you follow the Golden Rule, there is a lot that you would not do and there is a lot that you *would* do. You would not be rude to other people and you would be more likely to be kind and polite. You would have the kind of manners that would make you shine for Jesus.

**Following the Golden Rule will help to make you
more thoughtful. Do you agree?** _____

B. Read the poem at Appendix C. We think this would
be a nice poem for you to copy on the computer, or
print nicely on a colored piece of paper. Hang the poem up in
your room and memorize it. Your parents probably know the
Golden Rule. They will help you to understand these things
even better.

Being a Witness

As we near or come to the end of the month, we are going to talk about being a witness. A **witness** is someone who tells what he knows about a matter. A witness is always supposed to tell the truth. He is to tell the facts. People who know and love Jesus are to be witnesses for Him. Children who will be bright gems for His crown will surely tell others about Him. Children, as well as grown-ups, need to pray for the help of the Holy Spirit if they are to witness for the Savior. The facts that Jesus' witnesses need to tell are found in the Bible. You need to read and learn the Bible to be a good witness. Whenever you can, try to find some way to tell what you know about the Lord Jesus.

When You Pray

In Acts 1:8, Jesus has promised that the Holy Spirit will help God's people to witness for Him in nearby and faraway places. Pray that God will help you to be a part of this great work.

Devotionals for Each Month

1. Children Can Witness
2. Fishers of Men
3. Witness to All People

MONTH 1

Children Can Witness

2 Kings 5:1–4

A. You just read a small part of a story in the Bible that you might have heard before. It is about a man named Naaman who had the very bad disease of leprosy. **Leprosy** is a disease of the skin that is even worse than chicken pox. Chicken pox usually gets better, but leprosy gets worse. Naaman was a soldier in the land of Syria, and he was important to the king there. But did you notice something in verses 2 and 3? Naaman and his wife had a servant girl who had been brought there from the land of Israel. She told Naaman's wife that God's prophet could heal Naaman. Because of what this little girl said, the king sent Naaman to Israel and God used the prophet Elisha to heal him. Not only that, Naaman also came to believe in the one true God. This little girl had the courage to tell what she knew about God's power, and after that, look what happened! You are not too young to tell what you know about the things of God. If you do, who knows what God might do!

True or False:

The little girl in the story did not really do anything important. _____

B. A woman named Fanny Crosby wrote about the story of Jesus in a hymn we call "Tell Me the Story of Jesus." This hymn is often sung by children and it is a wonderful hymn to know. We hope you and your family can sing it tonight. Think and talk about the story of Jesus. Talk about how your family can tell this story to others. Also, we hope the Lord will help *you* to know in your heart how dear and precious the Lord Jesus is and what a wonderful work He has done for sinners. And may He give you courage like He gave to Naaman's little servant girl.

MONTH 2

Fishers of Men

Mark 1:16–20

A. Many people like to go fishing. Maybe you know someone who likes to go fishing. Maybe even you do. When people go fishing, they go to catch fish, of course. In Jesus' day, those who were fishermen would catch the fish and sell them. That was their work. Simon and Andrew, as well as James and John, were fishermen. Jesus wanted these men to leave the work they usually did and come and follow Him as He traveled. The most important thing that He wanted of them was that they would become "fishers of men." That means He wanted them to go and "catch" people and bring them to the Kingdom of God. Jesus still wants His followers to do that. But how do you catch people? What Jesus means is that He wants us to tell others about Him and pray that the Holy Spirit will help them to believe in Him. You can do this even though you are young. Perhaps there is another child who lives near you who you can invite to church. They will hear about Jesus there. Maybe you can tell an unsaved aunt, uncle or cousin certain lessons you have been learning from the Bible. These are just a couple of the ways that you can be a fisher of men. You can probably think of other ways. Ask God to help you.

Circle the right word:

Jesus wants His followers to catch (fish / people).

B. Try to think of six ways you can be a fisher of men. Write each one down on an index card (or draw a picture for each). Put a paper clip on the top edge of each card. Put the cards in a box or in an empty wastebasket. Then, ask a parent or someone older to help you make a fishing pole: Take about three or four feet of string and attach a magnet to one end. Tie the other end of the string onto a stick or pole. Now, you will "fish" for one of the cards in the container, using your fishing pole. Which one did you get? That is what you will try to do this week, if it is okay with your parents. Maybe next week you can go "fishing" again. Don't forget to pray!

MONTH 3

Witness to All People

Matthew 28:16–20

A. Have you ever heard these verses before? There is a good chance that you have. They contain a command that Jesus gave to His people. He gave this command after He rose from the dead and a short time before He returned to His Father in Heaven. There are some very important words in these verses. In verses 18 through 20 are the words known as "The Great Commission." In The Great Commission, Jesus is commanding His followers to tell people from all over the world about His salvation. He is saying that we should teach them about Him and how they can be a part of His Church. He is saying that those who believe in Him should be taught His Word and how to live for Him. He is making a promise to help with this important work. You see, it is not just that it is *nice* to tell all these people about the need for salvation; it is what we have been *commanded* to do by the Lord Himself. How can you be a part of The Great Commission?

True or False:

Jesus saves people from all nations and languages.

_____

B. Get a globe or world map and bring it to family devotions. Stick little pins in the places you want to pray for. Special places would be the countries where there are missionaries that you know about or your church supports. The Christians working in those countries need prayer. You can do that. Lead your family in prayer for those countries. Then think about sending a card or note to some of these missionaries.

Following the Shepherd

Many times in the Bible, God's children are called His sheep. You know a little bit about sheep, don't you? Sheep need a lot of care. The person who takes care of them is called a **shepherd**. Jesus is *our* Shepherd. Those who love Him and belong to Him are His sheep. He is the *Good* Shepherd. He says so in John Chapter 10. If you belong to Jesus, then you are one of His lambs and you must follow Him. There is no other way to sparkle and shine than to follow your Shepherd. The Lord Jesus, our dear Shepherd, takes very good care of us. We have already talked about the fact that He gave His life for His sheep. He also has given us a special day and has given us the Church to help us to follow Him and to help direct us in the right way. If He is to be our Shepherd, we must always, always put Him first and worship Him alone.

When You Pray

Pray for these things: "Lord Jesus, help me to be a trusting and obedient lamb who does not wander. Keep me safe and show me the way you want me to go. Please help me to love you above all else."

Devotionals for Each Month

1. The Shepherd's Care
2. The Sabbath Day/Church
3. God is God Alone

MONTH 1

The Shepherd's Care

Psalm 23

A. It certainly would be nice if you would hide this psalm in your heart. Maybe you have done that already. This is the best-known psalm. Most Christians love it and you can understand why. It was written by David, who had been a shepherd before he became king of Israel. The psalm is teaching us what God is like as our Shepherd. Since the Lord Jesus is also God, whatever this psalm says about our Shepherd is true of Him, as well as our Heavenly Father. This wonderful psalm is teaching us about God's care and how our Shepherd provides for our needs. David speaks here of how he did not fear evil and anyone who loves God can say the same thing. Something else we learn from David is that the Shepherd will help us to be good if we follow Him. That is what it means when it says He leads us in the paths of righteousness. Remember one day when we talked about the "path of the wicked"? If you have the Lord as your Shepherd, you will follow Him through His Word and He will lead you away from the path of the wicked. And the best thing is that His goodness and mercy will always be with you.

Fill in the answers:

Who wrote this psalm? _____ Who was his Shepherd? _____

B. Pick your favorite verse in Psalm 23 and make a picture of it: On a piece of construction paper, draw a shepherd and a lamb. Make a very nice picture, using your colored pencils. Maybe you have some stickers that you could add to your picture, or cotton balls for clouds, or you could cut out shapes to glue on. Of course, you would want to let your parents see this picture. Think about this after your picture is finished: Is Jesus *your* Shepherd? Is He caring for *you* like the shepherd is caring for the lamb in your picture?

MONTH 2

The Sabbath Day/Church

Exodus 20:8–11

A. We are now going to talk about something that God gave us to help us follow Him: He gave us a special day to rest and worship Him. When God created the world, He made it in six days and He rested on the seventh day. This is what God wants us to do. He wants us to work hard for six days and then rest from our work on one day out of seven. On that one day, He wants us to enjoy Him and His works. Sometimes, we call this day of rest the Sabbath Day and sometimes we call it the Lord's Day. In the fourth commandment, God teaches that this day is to be kept holy. Sunday is the Christian's Sabbath Day. On Sunday we should go to church and worship God with His people. We should be very happy to go to church and, when we are there, we should try to be on our best behavior. It is the most special thing that we do all week. We should honor our great God and our loving Savior by keeping His day holy and special and by showing that church is a special place. In church, we should listen carefully to the sermons and the prayers and the Bible readings. We should sing the hymns and give of our gifts of money. Honoring the Lord, Sunday after Sunday, will help us to follow Him on our journey to Heaven. And when

God's children someday reach Heaven, it will be like a Sabbath that has no end.

Fill in the word:

The most important thing we do each week is to go to

_____.

B. You may not be able to do this today, but we suggest that you get a book on the life of Eric Liddell or view the movie about him. The movie is called *Chariots of Fire*. It is possible that you know his story already. How did this man honor the Lord's Day? What did the Lord do for him? Think about yourself and how you honor the Lord's Day. We hope that you go to church, for one thing. We hope that you honor the Lord in your behavior at church, and we hope that you use this special day to rest and worship God and help others.

MONTH 3

God is God Alone

Exodus 20:1–3

A. We decided that a good place to close out these devotionals would be at the first commandment, which you just finished reading. You see, when you think about following the Good Shepherd, you must remember that you are always to put Him first. You must love and worship God alone and you must always put *Him* above all else. That is what you learn from this commandment. More than any other thing, we want you to remember that the Lord Jesus is the best treasure you could possibly have. He alone is the way to be saved. Without Him, you cannot go to Heaven. What do you want to be when you grow up? Do you want to be a farmer, a banker, a doctor, a fireman, or a wife and mother? Or something else? No matter what kind of work you do when you grow up, we want you to be sure of one important thing: that all of your life you obey the first commandment. Make sure that all of your life you follow Jesus and that *He* is the One you love the most. And if He is, some great and wonderful day He will gather *you* as a bright gem for His crown.

B. Tonight, sing with your family the song "When He Cometh," by W. O. Cushing. After you sing, pray with your parents. Ask God to teach you about Jesus and how to live for Him. Ask Him to help you to love and worship Him alone. And may He bless you all of your life.

Appendix A

Two and One

I have two ears and only one mouth
The reason, I think, is clear
It teaches me that it will not do
To talk about all I hear.

I have two eyes and only one mouth;
The reason of this must be,
That I should learn it will not do
To talk about all I see.

I have two hands and only one mouth;
And it is worth repeating:
The two are for work that I need to do—
The one is for eating.

Appendix B

Do good

Do all the good you can
By all the means you can,
In all the ways you can
In all the places you can,
At all the times you can,
To all the people you can,
As long as ever you can.

—John Wesley

Appendix C

To do to others as I would
That they should do to me,
Will make me gentle, kind and good,
As children ought to be.

This book is dedicated
to my grandchildren
who have not yet come.

Psalm 102:18

**This will be written for the
generation to come,
That a people yet to be created
may praise the LORD.**

Order Information

*For additional copies of this book or for a brochure
of other available products, contact:*

SPEAKABLE GIFTS
17 Elridge Lane
Willingboro, NJ 08046

Phone number: 609 871-6433
email: *SpeakableGifts@juno.com*

*Also, call or email for information on wholesale pricing
for bookstore and church orders.*

Copies of this book may also be obtained from:

ESSENCE PUBLISHING
at *www.essencebookstore.com*
or phone 1-800-238-6376

CPSIA information can be obtained at www.ICGtesting.com
Printed in the USA
BVOW02s0244180116

433210BV00001B/69/P